ARTIFACTS

ARTIFACTS

AN ARCHAEOLOGIST'S YEAR IN SILICON VALLEY

CHRISTINE FINN

The MIT Press   Cambridge, Massachusetts   London, England

First MIT Press paperback edition, 2002

© 2001 Massachusetts Institute of Technology

This book was set in Garamond 3, Futura, and Arial by Graphic
Composition, Inc., Athens, Georgia.

Printed and bound in the United States of America.

Library of Congress Cataloging-in-Publication Data

Finn, Christine.
 Artifacts : an archaeologist's year in Silicon Valley / Christine Finn.
  p.   cm.
 Includes bibliographical references and index.
 ISBN 0-262-06224-0 (hc. : alk. paper), 0-262-56154-9 (pb)
 1. Santa Clara Valley (Santa Clara County, Calif.)—Civilization—20th
century. 2. Santa Clara Valley (Santa Clara County, Calif.)—Description
and travel. 3. Santa Clara Valley (Santa Clara County, Calif.)—Social life
and customs—20th century. 4. Material culture—California—Santa
Clara Valley (Santa Clara County) 5. Technological innovations—Social
aspects—California—Santa Clara Valley (Santa Clara County)
6. Computers—Social aspects—California—Santa Clara Valley (Santa
Clara County) 7. Technology and civilization. 8. Finn, Christine—
Journeys—California—Santa Clara Valley (Santa Clara County)
9. Archaeologists—California—Santa Clara Valley (Santa Clara
County)—Biography. I. Title.

F868.S25 F56   2001
979.4'73—dc21   2001030660

Photo credits are found on page 224.

The book is dedicated to pioneers everywhere,
and to those who believe in them.

And to my father, who taught me how to see things.

CONTENTS |

PREFACE |

This started out as a book about things and it rapidly became a book about people—a certain group of people in a particular part of the world that has no map coordinate, common language or culture, but a unique commonality in being a mother lode of technological innovation unlike anywhere else on earth.

The book considers how the population of this enigmatic place is responding to changes they have initiated, or have had forced upon them. It looks at lateral connections between parts of the past and present that matter today to those working and living in the unique "SiVa" environment, and will matter tomorrow to a wider audience considering Silicon Valley in the broader scheme of cultural history.

In an essay published in 1942, William F. Ogburn stated: "The electronic digital computers that perform the seemingly magical functions of an electrical brain are an extraordinarily complex invention; yet they may call forth less adjusting than the simple invention of the wheel." What is crucial to understanding Silicon Valley today is not so much the amount of change, but the rate of change. It seemed to me that one way of examining this was to apply a combination of perceptions—the eye of a foreigner with the "what if" probing of the archaeologist. As L. P. Hartley noted, "the past is a foreign country." It was a simple enough approach six months ago, but the rapid escalation of change brought about by economic uncertainty in the tech industry created a new set of data. In attempting to make sense of this oscillating SiVa culture, I was in danger of never completing this book. So what I offer is a series of snapshots, some of which I hope offer up foundation material for further, more systematic academic study.

This is not a book of computer history, which is richly served already, but it is an attempt to offer an alternative perspective from a field that seems at odds with high technology and the future. But technological changes are key in the exploration and evaluation of ancient societies and artifacts, whether the development of stone tools, or transportation, or writing. One stage can be viewed as a precursor to another. And the compounding of these changes, the ways people respond to increasing complexities, or demands to "keep up" with technology, is the subject of much deliberation among sociologists, economists, and anthropologists. Increasingly archaeologists are also joining the debate, applying the same forensic scrutiny we use to view ancient cultures to the contemporary world.

In contemporary archaeology, people and things are no longer viewed as separate entities; things are related to people, and "material culture" is a name for things that are understood to be socialized, that is, put in a cultural context.

The way we categorize these things is related to the way we use them, or think about them, and understanding these two processes is often problematic if the people are no longer around to explain intention or meaning. Hence the long and heated debates in archaeology about things classified as "mother goddess" figures, or "votive offerings"—the quote marks here are not attempting to make a value judgment, but to suggest a category. And if people related to these objects were indeed still around, they may not necessarily speak, or think, the same language—culturally, intellectually, or philosophically—as anthropologists and ethnographers contend. For example, I do not know if your notion of an empty glass is the same as mine. If it is half-full (or half-empty) the problem is compounded.

So, I will not present a thesis on material culture; there are plenty of highly challenging books already on that. But I was interested in the way a computer, for example, is a useful tool, a machine to be junked, and a collectors' item in a space of time shorter than anything I'd encountered in any other context. I decided to use the computer as a way of getting into a discussion about changing value over time; about the way people personalize machines and, at the other extreme, collect them. They have been transformed by people into something with a different meaning from before.

And moving on to things, and the rest of the book title "artifacts"—or @rtifacts—are things that have been made for a purpose. We make and use things we need as part of our social lives. We make things for eating, for ritual, and for relaxation. We make things to shelter us, to keep us warm, to cool us down. When we can't find the things we need, we innovate and reshape. When we can't find the things we desire, we use a variety of senses to create them. We produce other things to capture memories, reproduce images, replay sounds. And when we think we've reached the peak of possibility, visionaries remind us that we are limited only by our imaginations.

It took millions of years and possibly as many incremental transformations to develop stone tool technology to the stage of recognizable arrowheads and scrapers. The first tools, those formed by *Homo habilis* (or "Handy Man") in Africa 2.5 million years ago. Identification of earlier forms comes with a caveat. Hammerlike blows can be the result of natural causes, such as heat, frost, or impact. An expert can identify the tell-tale "bulb of percussion" on cruder tools, while the certain intervention of human activity comes with more complex shaped or retouched flints. Here, the mind's eye has helped the hand to engineer one side of a leaf-shaped arrowhead to replicate the other, bending stone in a mirror image. With intensification of technology over time, the use of stone and flint is complemented and eventually superseded, in

most respects, by the use of synthetic materials—such as metal
and pottery. The management of fire, the organization of labor, and
the trade in raw materials finally heave the matful of humans off
the top of the helter-skelter, and on a twisting-turning path of
overwhelming complexity.

In the first place, such complexity was tempered by the passage
of time; human society gradually conditioned itself to the pace of
change, as hunter-gatherers became settled, trading routes became
established, cultural nodes developed. But all the while people's
horizons were broadening, there came an expectation to move
faster, to know more, to become more diverse, to feel comfortable
in the world and not just their settlement, hometown, or country.
In the past one hundred and fifty years, trains, planes, and automobiles have intensified the rate of movement of human beings and
their associated things, and as a result, their expectations. In his
study of the impact of the railway in Europe and the United States,
the New York writer Wolfgang Shivelbusch found evidence of
trauma, commuter stress, and various psychoses among the travelers in nineteenth-century railway carriages. Here their gazes were
not dwelling on gently rolling hills in quiet contemplation, as we
might believe from our contemporary perspective. Instead, they
were snagging their retinas on jagged fragments of images passing
by the picture windows at great speed.

The things humans created, consumed, or owned were also
bowing and distorting under the pressure of change. It was not
only possible, but also desirable, to be acquisitive, to have more
things. They were the tangible signs of status. In eighteenth-
century Europe, the journey around France, Greece, Italy, and Asia
Minor, better known as "The Grand Tour," demarcated those who
had leisure time, money to spare for travel and collecting, and the
classical knowledge to put it all into context. In nineteenth-
century Paris, Haussman's grand schemes for the city included

finely designed shopping malls, as well as railway stations each with the ever-prominent edifice of a vast clock, so that no one would be late. The malls, called arcades, were seductive and reminded those who had not of those who had. In the United States, the transcontinental railway opened up vistas which, as well as natural beauty, offered the seduction of betterment, the possibilities of movement to a new place to call home. Before too long, the interstates and freeways offered those who could drive (and afford to) a personal freedom to journey these terrains in the luxury of their own space, and at their own speed.

And what has all this to do with computers? Precisely, the sum of the above. Innovation in technology, driven by a consumer market and a desire to push the envelope of possibility; the response of those outside the industry to the things created in it, and how that reveals itself in other cultural patterns and change. A response to speed as seen in expectations in the workplace and at home, and the journey between; a sense that whatever one has is instantly superseded by the next new thing, and the effect this has on values in a social and economic sense. Archaeologists study change over time, and in Silicon Valley, such change is observable laterally, in a sweep of technology that spreads out from the software and hardware hothouses, down what remains of rural roads and open fields, and into the world. In this region alone, its effect can be felt by those aware of the white heat of the Valley from the edge of things. José, who used to pick cherries but now helps recycle silicon chips, Thelma, who makes more babysitting the children of a post-IPO couple than she did in a factory job, and Bob, who has made enough money from the sale of his mobile home to incoming techies, to live his twilight years a happy man in another state.

The modern material culture of Silicon Valley is driven by technology, but it encompasses architecture, clothing, transportation, entertainment, food, intercultural exchanges, and rituals. The way people are working and adapting, becoming wealthy, or barely getting by is visible in the cultural landscape of the fifteen cities that make up the area called "Silicon Valley."

One of the early "travelogues" of the area was *Siliconnections,* published in 1986. Its author, the pioneering engineer Forrest Mims, described the book as a "Cook's tour of what I have seen and observed" in thirty years in Silicon Valley. For Mims, who helped to develop the first personal computer, the Altair 8800, it was a book of adventures, written as much for the nontechnical reader as for those in the industry.

I wouldn't claim to match Mims's expertise, but what I am offering up is a kind of Cook's tour of my own, a brief one, and from the perspective of an archaeologist as foreign correspondent. The journey sometimes was as random as a literal in a search engine, and invariably led to other, fascinating turns. As an archaeologist I was not looking to excavate in the physical sense. Instead I was thinking about how much meaning we could make of the area as it is just now, as I write, with all its parallel changes over time. If the input of people, their anecdotes and histories, was taken away, and we just had things to interpret, what could we say? It was an exercise in what could be called "the Pompeii effect," and it's a fun game to play. What if Silicon Valley was covered in volcanic dust, higher than the highest building, so the De Anza Hotel sign in San Jose became a landmark on the ground? What would be made of the cars on the freeways, where old Buicks and the new Boxsters run together; or the elegantly designed high-tech campuses with multi-cultural themes; or the stunning, huge houses that seemed to have only one occupant. My methodology was simple; I drove around, walked, talked, asked questions, and kept a journal with paper and pen.

But during my months of research, Silicon Valley remained whimsical—dot.coms fell from ascendancy, stock markets panicked, house prices appeared to stabilize, then the NASDAQ picked up, prices rose, and so on. Without a cabin in the mountains to retreat to, I did my writing in a variety of locations: from a photography studio, a variety of cafes, libraries. The first words were penned from a desk in a start-up in Saratoga. The company dealt in on-line trading and wireless connections, and so this book began to take shape in a suitably ethereal environment. The moving and shaking, the constant flux, was quite deliberate. In first attempting to organize this mercurial material in a traditional academic way, I had begun to lose the thrill of discovery. I needed to remain on the edge, and rattling out the words in the company of other thrill-seekers—daytraders, venture capitalists, coders, and other addicts of the Valley's relentless buzz—seemed entirely appropriate.

I venture to offer up a book that is both a personal story and a shared one—a nontechie, non-American's take on Silicon Valley, and the places, things, and people found along the way.

January 2001

ACKNOWLEDGMENTS |

My indebtedness spreads far and wide, temporally and geographically.

Sellam Ismail was the navigator without whom I could never have undertaken such a journey into the unknown. This is as much Sellam's book as mine. He and Dag Spicer shared their insights of computer history with unbounding generosity. I am grateful to Tom Jackiewicz for our first of many conversations, and to Mark Jones for flying into San Francisco and not Los Angeles.

I thank the many people I interviewed—those named in the book, and others who gave me glimpses of Silicon Valley life in a series of brief encounters, at coffee shops, on train rides, and in grocery store lines.

Also those who let me use photographs, or took them for me, and shared their passion at the Vintage Computer Festivals and classic technology forums, among them John Honniball and Kurt Bangert, Hans Franke, and Zoran Stancic, who invited me to speak on tech artifacts in Slovenia. At Stanford University, Henry Lowood, Tim Lenoir, and Mark Granovetter gave me primers on Silicon Valley's history and structure, J. B. Shank gave me his own take on archaeology. Thanks to Diane Maxwell and Susan Landauer at San Jose MOMA, Elisabeth O'Connell at the Rosicrucian Museum, Joint Venture, Robert Z. Apte, Matt and Jacqueline Burnett, Dawn Corry, Howard Dyckoff, Mark Samis, and Rod Stetzer for their interest. Claudia Leschuck and Kenneth W. Rendell deserve applause for nailing the seemingly impossible. Doug McKnight let me in on Silicon Valley Business at KICU TV36, while the *San Jose Mercury News* was an invaluable resource in hand and on the web. And for the numerous other ethereal places tapped into and tripped over while writing this book, I thank their—often anonymous—authors.

I am grateful to those who gave me a workplace—Tin's Folded Ice-cream in downtown Saratoga, Bullpen Books, the Novel Cafe in Santa Monica, and to others who loaned me a couch, a car, or a cell phone. I thank Woody Lewis, Kathryn Klar, Steve Northup, Lynette Lithgow, and Dominic Pearson, for their real and virtual support in the United States, Peter Young and Elizabeth Himelfarb at *Archaeology* magazine, and Barbara DuMoulin and Eric Zarakov at Foveon.

In Oxford, my students on the ASA Program honed my fascination with America; Simon Morley, Tracey Kay and their team at STA Travel, never failed to get me there. Also Godfrey Hodgson, Neville Maxwell, and the Reuter Journalist Fellowship, which helped me start my own voyage of discovery ten years ago, and continued to provide professional sustenance. I also acknowledge my colleagues at the Institute of Archaeology—where the book's proposal, and its last words, were written on a computer in a Georgian building, atop Henry II's great hall, atop a Bronze Age burial ground. The encouragement and friendship of Barry Cunliffe, Martin Henig, Nigel Henbest, Emma Pryke—who all read and commented on the text—Heather Couper, Susan and James Hill, John Hyman, Rebekah Lee, Ruth Ling, Christine Peters, Derek Roe, the Shaw family, Lauren Soertsz, and Lorraine Wild proved priceless. Thank you to John Jeff, for Silicon Valley '84.

And at MIT Press, my gratitude goes to Judy Feldmann and designer Emily Gutheinz, Vicki Jennings, Christine Dunn, Gita Manaktala, Ann Rae Jonas, Katherine Innis, Ann Sexsmith, Ann Twiselton, and the rest of the team in London and Cambridge, Massachusetts. And not least of all, I am indebted to my commissioning editors, Larry Cohen and Bob Prior, without whose faith there would probably be no book. They fostered my idea and, when events moved swiftly around me, encouraged the book's own change over time. For that, not least, my thanks is insanely great.

PHOTO ESSAY

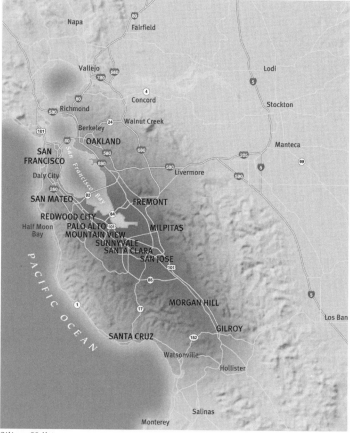

Silicon Valley.

San Jose Mercury News ad, 2000. Photo by William Howard.

Orchard, Santa Clara Valley.

Prune packing, Santa Clara Valley.

Olson's cherries, Sunnyvale, September 2000.

Hewlett-Packard garage, Palo Alto.

Yahoo! sign, San Francisco, 2000.

Yahoo! sign, New York City.

"Bunny suit."

Great America, Santa Clara.

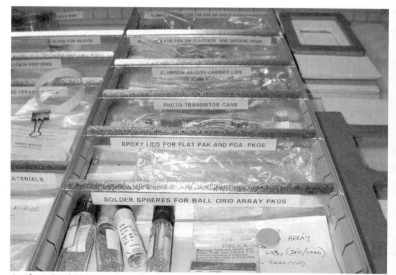

Artifacts, Intel Museum, Santa Clara.

Mantle trinkets, Tom Jackiewicz's apartment, San Jose, January 2000.

Sculpture by David Middlebrook, Westin Hotel, Palo Alto. Photo by David Middlebrook.

Artist with Apple ad, Los Angeles, May 2000.

Familia-Y-Vida health mural, Alviso.

Bayside Canning Co., Alviso.

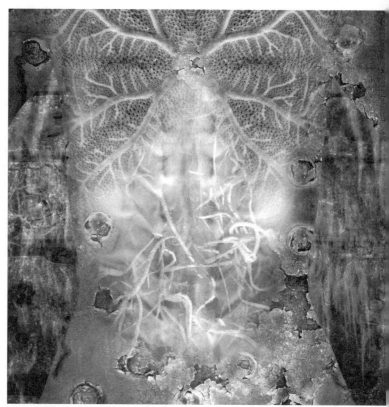

"Surgery Flat," Julieanne Kost. Photo by Julieanne Kost/Adobe.

Painted Highway, Silicon Valley.

Rosicrucian Egyptian Museum, San Jose, September 2000.

Rosicrucian Egyptian Museum entrance, San Jose.

Mycenean columns, Treasury of Atreus, Greece, artist's impression, early twentieth century.

Sistrum. Artifact number RC1765, Rosicrucian Egyptian Museum, San Jose.

Rosicrucian Egyptian Museum, San Jose.

Fry's Electronics, store exterior, Campbell, May 2000.

San Jose Mercury News ad. Photo by William Howard.

Old house, Alviso, August 2000.

House for Sale, Hicks Road, Los Gatos. Photo by Ian McRae.

Archive photograph, Alviso Yacht Club.

Cover of Skinner's technology sale catalog, April 1, 2000.

Ad for Honeywell's Kitchen Computer, from the archives of The Computer History Museum Center.

J. Presper Eckert (on left) with ring counter from ENIAC.

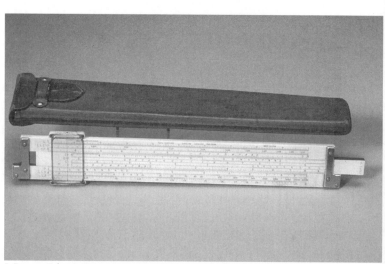

J. Presper Eckert's slide rule.

DEC equipment and ephemera, John Lawson's house, Malibu Hills.

Computer kit, from Sellam Ismail's vintage computer collection.

Recycling chute, San Jose. Photo by Tony Cole.

Cable, recycler's, San Jose. Photo by Tony Cole.

Recycled metal ingots. Photo by Tony Cole.

Recycling chips. Photo by Tony Cole.

Circuit board, recycler's, San Jose. Photo by Tony Cole.

Salvaged gold pieces, recycler's, San Jose. Photo by Tony Cole.

San Jose Mercury News ad, 2000. Photo by William Howard.

Oak tree, San Jose, September 2000.

THE PLACE

THE WAY TO SAN JOSE |

The flight to San Jose was packed. I had been bumped off a plane from Phoenix to Oakland, and there had been six of us at the airline desk begging for the last seats of the night to anywhere near San Francisco. One guy said he was seeing a liver transplant specialist; a young woman in a wheelchair had already checked in her luggage containing her medication, which was even then heading to Oakland. I was meeting a friend I hadn't seen for twenty years. He was flying in from Sydney to San Francisco at 7 A.M., and his plane was expected early. Naturally. Clutching my boarding pass like a winning lottery ticket, I was wedged in a back row seat between one man reading *Harry Potter,* and another in a black leather jacket who was poking a finger at his Palm Pilot. The Potter fan ended a chapter, and in conversation I discovered he worked in semiconductors. The other guy was staring at his screen with increasing intensity as we prepared for take off. With a heavy sigh, he shut the machine down. "That's cute," I said, "How long has it been out?" His reply came with a broad grin. "It comes out tomorrow. I designed the email for it." "Amazing," I thought, unaware that of all the passengers on the plane for San Jose, I was probably the only one not involved in the computer industry. I was a true "cybernaif," for whom the next twelve months would be one big learning curve. But that night, San Jose was just a city in northern California, a place in a song title, and a destination closer to San Francisco International than the airline's other option, Orange County.

The Palm Pilot owner was Tom Jackiewicz, and I am eternally grateful that when he could have feigned deafness, foreignness, or deep sleep, he in fact answered my quick-fire questions, barely losing his smile or his grip on the handheld computer. It turned out he received several hundred emails a day—a staggering revelation to someone whose inbox was still comfortably lined with old friends' messages, nostalgically retained there as if they had been tied with ribbon and kept in an antique box. If they could gather dust they would shower the air each time I logged on. I could barely master sending an attachment. But for the next hour or so, here was my chance to find out everything I had ever wanted to know about email but had been much too afraid to ask.

The truth is, I'd had some bad times with computers, which would run variations along the lines of swallowing, freezing,

Tom Jackiewicz, January 2000.

deleting, or downright annihilating my texts. Some years ago, when first shown how to cut and paste, I was thrown into such a frenzy of confusion I began to interlace documents with others apparently plucked from the depths of the hard disc at random. On the floor of a university computer room, I literally used scissors and sticky tape to prepare documents that I had earlier cut, pasted, and then rearranged into chaos on screen. I'd hear tales of other disasters and weave them into my thesis nightmares. "My daughter," confided one Oxford professor, "lost all the spaces between the words of her dissertation . . ." Another friend, red eyed from lack of sleep, whispered: "It took everything. I went to print out, and it was all gone . . ."

It hadn't always been that way. In 1984 I had made my first visit to California, and had driven through Silicon Valley with someone self-trained in an escalating career field called "computer programming." If I don't recall the geography of the place as I saw it then, the associated words run in my brain like a mantra—C, Ada, Cobol, Fortran, Operating Systems, DEC PDP11, IBM . . ." You'd make a good programmer," the friend said, though I can't think for what reason. But partly to impress him, I went to evening classes offered in "BASIC" held once a week at an old market town in southeast England called Sandwich. There were about a dozen of us seated at school desks there to learn the rudiments of "high-level programming." It perplexed me that something called "high-level" was in fact the lowest form of programming life. But those amoeba-like beginnings set something glowing in the Petrie dish; although hopeless at math, I found the logic of zeros and ones quite compelling. I became fascinated by the leaps of technology involved, and the sheer romance of a nineteenth-century poet's daughter giving her name to a U.S. computer defense language.

Had I actually left journalism then for a career in computing, this would be a very different story. As it was, I bought the BASIC

books, completed the course, and promptly did nothing more
about it. But within six years, I was experiencing computers in the
workplace, as typesetting evolved from hot metal to web-offset and
editing on screen. In 1976, when I began work as a local newspaper reporter at sixteen, we thumped out our stories on old Rem-
ingtons or Coronas, the typesetters clacked out the words in lead,
we checked the long galley proofs, and made alterations by hand.
Within ten years, on another newspaper, the typesetters input copy
on screen and we checked for typos on a made-up page; by 1990,
in a television newsroom, we not only input scripts by means of a
specially designed program, but content output was computerized
and the news video tapes played in preprogrammed sequence.
Later, at university, I began the transition of thinking about own-
ing a computer, agonized about it for several years, and bought
two second-hand Apples, an LCIII and a Powerbook. I went to
computer classes, but producing the text for my doctoral thesis
was still the stuff of nightmares. At a place like Oxford, where
examination scripts are still hand-written, and in some cases,
books, I found comfort in an environment that allowed for dissent-
ing voices among the swelling ranks of the computerati. But I
wasn't entirely convincing in my rage against the machine. There
was still something about those zeros and ones, the odd collusion
of science and art expressed in Jacquard looms and textiles, Ada's
poetic passion, and the philosophical consequences of machines
that could think.

   On that flight to San Jose, and for days after, I mused on all
this; seeking something to connect it on a personal level. Somewhere in Berkeley, in a scruffy diner, the answer came. On the
countertop was a dog-eared copy of the magazine *Fast Company,*
and as I waited for breakfast I found an article in which a Japanese
visionary predicted that someday computers would be in museums. As an archaeologist, this was so blindingly applicable that

my pancakes cooled in the frenzy of my writing something down. Three months later, in the first days of 2000, I came back to Silicon Valley. And this is where the story really begins.

January 2000. Somewhere in Silicon Valley, I am waiting in the drizzle for a bus that will take me to a train, and another bus—or was it train? And eventually I will get to the in-house museum of one of the biggest players in the computer industry—Intel Corporation. But for now, I am watching and waiting. A coach shoots by, showering me with gray specks, and from the windows peer rows of faces. I wonder if they are prospective computer engineers, or tourists trying to find Silicon Valley; either way they seem fascinated to see people standing on the pavement, at a bus stop by a freeway, in the middle of a vast industrial site.

In months to come, I will look back on this journey and come to bless the lack of foresight on my part that led to my taking public transport instead of a rental car from Berkeley to Santa Clara. The journey takes me two and a half hours, instead of fifty minutes by car. I chat with a bus driver, another passenger at the bus stop, and a young guy on a train. And in that time I am made aware of one crucial thing—there are people in this place called Silicon Valley who do not own multimillion-dollar homes, do not sit on red-hot stock options, do not have new start-ups, wait for IPOs, drive top-of-the-range Ferraris, do not even own a computer let alone a computer company. For them, the extraordinary, exponential rate of change in the landscape is not part of their personal landscape. To them, this is still the Santa Clara Valley, and to those who can recall fifty years back, it's "The Valley of Heart's Delight," and, in their memory's eye, one of the most glorious and bountiful places in America.

Today's Silicon Valley bears the traces of those rurally halcyon days in place and streets names such as the Pruneyard, Blossom Hill Road; in the same way it has taken on the marks of its new cultural identity—Woz Way. Traces of past and future past, which await the context of narratives. The change is just discernible, as lateral movement that transforms orchards into apartments, pumpkin fields into high energy fields, stables and stores into storehouses of ideas and warehouses of hardware; a feast of electrons, where baskets once overspilled with apples and apricots.

It was José, a bus driver for the Valley Transport Authority, who was the first person to say to me the immortal words: "I remember when it was all orchards round here." In his late thirties or early forties, Jose's recollections sounded out in the empty bus like the words of a wise, old man. When he was growing up, he said, he could take fruit from the trees all the time. At night he could look out over the lights of San Jose and identify its landmarks with ease. "There was a tall building which used to have a green light on it." He looked puzzled. "They don't turn it on anymore. I don't know why." Spanish-speaking José was one of Silicon Valley's unsung pioneer workers. In the early 1970s he worked in the first wave of high-tech industry, disassembling and reassembling computers. Then he left to work as a bus driver for the VTA. His friend stayed on at the company. "He's pretty well off," José said. "But I'm content. I'm my own boss, I like talking to people." He pointed out the hills where he bought a house five years ago. "I couldn't afford the same one now." Today there were more beggars around, and more scams. José said he was duped by a "homeless" man with a three-year-old child standing at the side of road. "I took him back to my place to give him some work in the garden. Gave him $40. He took my pager. Had to pay $20 to get it back from the dealer he had sold it to." Sure, there were more jobs, but Santa Clara Valley was a different place these days. He pointed out my next bus stop. "Archaeology is so interesting," he said. "It's good to look at where we've come from—to know that this isn't it . . ."

Two people at the bus stop. One turns down his barely visible microradio to talk to me. Josh is a twenty-year-old laborer who lives in a trailer home in Santa Clara. The rent is $1200 a month, which he shares with his sister. It's an insecure existence. "There's so much pressure on park owners to sell out," he says. Josh works on a building site and studies at a tech college. For five years, skateboards have been his passion. He dreams of being in business, of having $20,000 to buy the special equipment to make customized models. Although all the new concrete gives him places to skateboard, he gets turned off these places by the police. Now he says he despises the changes. I spot my bus a block away and I ask Josh if I can keep in touch, ask him more about growing up in Silicon Valley. "Your email address would be great," I say. He gives a wry smile. "I don't have email, and no computer—though I know what I want to know about them." He is thoughtful. "If I could use new technology to make the world a better place then I would be in favor of it." He remains unconvinced by the culture around him. "I can remember the orchards . . . ," he says as his music listening is interrupted by ads for dot.coms.

Late morning, and I am one of the few on public transport in Santa Clara. At the train station, I get talking to Jeff, a twenty-year-old computer programmer. Correct that—a retired twenty-year-old computer programmer. Good looking, open, and articulate, Jeff has programmed since he was fifteen while at high school and at college. His father works in the computer industry at Seattle. "I was courted by Microsoft when I was a lot younger," Jeff adds with a flourish. There's a pause and he says: "I resisted." He seems oblivious to the strangeness of this concept—a teenage prime-time in which retirees are barely in their twenties and can carve out a couple more careers if they want to. Now Jeff wants out of the industry to travel and, more than that, to get away from the culture around him. He reckons he made $150,000 last year and spent the lot on "experiences and fair-weather friends." He fixes me with a look that is only half-serious. "I've wised up," he says. "I'm not convinced by the priorities of my peers." Jeff lives near Huntington Beach, south of Los Angeles. It's a surfers' paradise, but he doesn't like that lifestyle either. He has an e-company with his best friend in San Francisco. "He's very cool. I'm the optimist, he's the pessimist for a reality check." But he feels ready for a change. He just wants to travel; Florence would be good. On the train we talk about life, love, and the computer age. Jeff says he doesn't read much, but had just got into Herodotus. "If you like meeting interesting people you should check out Burning Man," he says. "It's a wild art festival in Nevada—artists burn their work as a finale." He says the idea of temporariness appeals to him.

Within the Robert Noyce building of Intel Corporation, the Intel Museum in Santa Clara was to be my initiation into Silicon Valley's corporate culture, and the way the technological past is presented to the outside world. It is busy with a school group working its way through the pieces of silicon, the stages of wafer and chip production, colorful storyboards, hands-on displays. The artifacts include turquoise smocks embroidered with flowers, ladybirds, and the peace symbol. They look startlingly out of context, but are examples of early workgear for those involved in chip manufacture or fabrication, commonly known as Fab. The suits date from the 1970s. Now Fab workers wear suits that look something like those worn in the nuclear industry; they protect the worker and the valuable chip. They are called "bunny suits" and cover the worker from head to toe. Apparently there are forty-seven steps to suiting up in Fab. They range from taking a drink of water to wash away throat particles to putting on the bunny suit without letting it touch the floor—"tuck bunny suit pant legs into bootees. . . ." Workers are reminded that "If one tiny speck of dust falls on a chip while it is being made, the chip has been ruined."

Miniature "BunnyPeople™" are on sale in the Intel Museum Store. They are produced in bright colors, and sell particularly well. Like hot chips, you could say. The Intel Museum Store is an important part of Intel's public image. There are decorative blankets and stationery items featuring a chip design. Richard, who works in the shop, displays a brighter face about life in Silicon Valley, which is where he grew up. He organizes all his social life on email. "Especially tennis matches."

There is a quote on the wall of the museum that seems to sum things up pretty much: "Working in Fab is like cycling through a revolving door. Just when you learn how to build one product, a newer one with all its technical challenges needs to be manufactured—better, cheaper and three months earlier than originally planned." The astute thoughts of Randy Phillips, Intel manufacturing manager.

Intel has been in business for thirty-three years and the company started up by Gordon Moore and Robert Noyce is the stuff of Silicon Valley legend. The objects collected in the corporate museum chart the story. Here, staff look after some 54,000 artifacts ranging from bits of chips to documentation—framed certificates, Intel literature, staff awards, photographs, original designs and plans. I am shown a technodinosaur, a personal computer weighing sixty pounds. There are discs housing samples of software used for machines driven by the Intel chip. The process of technology, as much as the tangible effects of it, is important here. The majority of people using a computer with "Intel Inside™" never see the chip. "This is a new industrial age—we can't just talk about it, we have to know how it works," says Rachel Stewart, a curator. So, engineers donate artifacts, and they usually come with a descrip-

"Witch in a bottle," Pitt Rivers Museum, Oxford.

tive label explaining not only how the item was made, but what it does and how in fact it fits in with the product's cultural history. One handwritten note reads: "variety of internal oxidized aluminum heat spheres" used "to help transfer heat for device to outer surfaces from packages, circa 1980s–90s." I'm reminded of the Pitt Rivers Museum at Oxford, a Victorian curiosity of museology, where many of the contents of cabinets and drawers have labels, handwritten in ink a century before—"This bottle contains a witch" being one of my favorites.

A few weeks later, I trace one of the handwritten notes back to a retired Intel engineer, George Chiu, at Palo Alto. We have breakfast in a glorious English-style garden created by his wife, Florence. George is certainly part of Silicon Valley history. He began his career in transistor packaging with Rheem semiconductors,

George Chiu, Palo Alto. Photo by Florence Chiu.

later bought by the giant Raytheon. From 1960 to 1968, he was at ~~Fairchild Semiconductor~~ in Mountain View. It was an exhilarating time to be working in semiconductors. "There was an explosion of technology" with the creative sparks flying off Fairchild's "immortal eight." "I consider Fairchild my university, " he says. The work pushed his creative skills to the limits and conversation with him identifies some of the dynamics behind the extraordinary Silicon Valley thrust. "We were always meeting constant changes, developing new skills." He was there for eight years before becoming employee number 39 at Intel's first headquarters in Middlefield Road. In those days people wore shirts and ties. It was a time of innovation in employment culture as well as technology. George was part of a new wave of multiculturalism; Intel hired a diversity of engineers—from China, Taiwan, and India. "I feel I was on the cutting edge." He stayed with the company for thirty years. When he retired he gave materials to the museum and gave his memories to Intel's oral history collection. George gives me a prototype package as a souvenir and while I ponder what pioneering engineers do when they retire, George takes me back outside to show me his latest project. It's a handsome garden studio, fashioned like an English cottage with paned windows and paneled door. This will be his den, and he's making it from scratch using mainly recycled materials. "It's a new challenge for me!" he says with a boyish glee one suspects lies in every one of the Silicon Valley old-school alumni.

I go to see another of the Fairchild old guard, Dan Boyd, who moved to Silicon Valley with his wife, Nan, from Texas, in 1961. They've stayed in the same house, guarded by their neighbor's straight-as-a-die palm tree, as the valley has grown and changed around them. Dan also worked for Raytheon and another pivotal

Dan and Nan Boyd, Palo Alto, May 2000.

company, Texas Instruments. He was in fabrication at Fairchild, and pretty much like engineers of modern Silicon Valley, moved between companies as the work and managements changed. He helped to set up projects in India, China, and the former Yugoslavia, and also helped train Chinese and Japanese engineers. At AMI he worked on information-storage devices—ISD—as part of the pioneering work to help chips "speak"—it's a technique used, among other places, on talking greetings cards.

Nan is also part of the Silicon Valley story. She has worked in market research in Santa Clara for twenty-two years. The prototype products today are invariably high-tech, such as computer games. "Where it used to be ladies talking about lettuce, it's now engineers testing software manuals!"

THE LONG THEN |

"Can you see anything?"

"Yes, wonderful things!"

—Famed conversation between the archaeologists Howard Carter and Lord Carnarvon on the opening of the tomb of Tutankhamun, the Valley of the Kings, Egypt, November 26, 1922

Once my eyes get accustomed to the light, I can make out the coffins, the sarcophagi, the walls decorated with Egyptian motifs of palms and papyrus. There are people wandering around, some distracted by the stunning sights and sounds; others are sitting cross-legged on the floor, discussing objects while in deep conversation. I look again at the walls. Egyptian figures carry goods, row boats. The cargo is regular in size. Rectangular boxes. They are marked with the same symbol: "Fry's."

Fry's Electrical Store in Campbell is one of the showcases of Silicon Valley architecture. Styled like an Egyptian temple, its interior continues the fantasy big-time. I would love to have been able to include a photograph of this remarkable edifice, but Fry's likes to maintain its secrecy on the store front. So, all I can say is, picture this. Upright mummy cases open to reveal boxes of software. Telephones are perched on fake tomb masonry. And the walls are a pastiche of hieroglyphs and scenes from everyday life 3500 years ago.

What makes this even more bizarre is that just a few miles down the road, another ancient Egyptian edifice confuses the landscape of Silicon Valley. The Rosicrucian Museum in San Jose is one of the best collections of Egyptian material in private hands. It is housed in a series of stunning buildings, complete with sphinxes, and other architectural devices, set in a small park. The public space also includes a statue of the Roman emperor Augustus.

Inside, the collection is extensive. The objects were acquired from the 1930s onwards. The place is billed as "the only Egyptian museum in the world authentically designed in the classical style of Ancient Egyptian temple architecture." The tie-in with the Rosicrucian order—with which Blaise Pascal, Isaac Newton, Francis Bacon, and Michael Faraday have been associated—is a complex area that relates to the spiritual philosophy associated with the ancient Egyptians. Suffice to say the contents of this archaeological museum are a counter to the world in which they now reside.

I am drawn to an object called a "sistrum." A sacred musical instrument that rattled when shaken. According to a caption beside the display case, the Roman writer Plutarch noted that the sistrum reminds us that things are constantly in motion, "being, as it were, aroused and stirred up . . . showing that when corruption was tied fast and brought to a standstill, generation again unlooses and restores nature by means of motion."

Archaeologists mediate between the past and the present, bringing things literally into the light, illuminating ancient worlds, and suggesting, though not offering inconclusive proof, other ways of being. It is a continual play between the known and the unknown. In the cyber world, it is down to those with access to the new technology and those without it.

A few years ago, I was visiting the Tombs of the Nobles near Luxor in Egypt. I was in a group of tourists looking at the tomb of a vintner. The subterranean space was small so we were split into two groups. I was in the first. We gingerly came down into the tomb where, in the light of a bare bulb, we could see the walls and ceiling were lush with paintings of grape vines, the tendrils insinuating their way into the fabric of the plaster. With the guide, I was last to turn my back on this image, and as I stepped on the ladder the lights went out. Pitch black. The next group was already beginning its descent and so the guide lit a match and found a small torch. I knew the dimensions of the tomb, but the newcomers edged and hesitated, bent double to avoid cracking their heads on the ceiling. I guided their heads upright where, in a manner more spectacular and revelatory than that of our group, they gasped in wonder at the fragments of paintwork. Was that a grapevine? And here? And look, again all over the walls! And the ceiling! Their illumination was less instant, more mysterious. More like Carter and Carnarvon gazing in wonder at the tomb of Tutankhamen.

I am left wondering how we excavate the web. How much is digging and how much a process of lateral connection?

In archaeology we consider geography, climate, and natural resources when we look at the beginnings of technology millennia ago. The so-called Holocene hot-spots, among them the comma-shaped Fertile Crescent of the Near East, that emerged after the last Ice Age and had environmental similarities. These were adequate water supplies and fertile soils encouraging the growth of food products that, in the next stage of technology, could be controlled or "domesticated" by human adaptation and innovation.

In the places where the first complex societies emerged around 5,000 years ago—China, the Indus Valley, Mesopotamia, Egypt—surplus food supplies and a growing but sustainable population helped to produce a beyond-needs situation—technology could be used for creative consumables such as decorated buildings and lavish tombs. Objects were made desirable by the inclusion of labor-intensive craftwork and imported materials. The new, new thing became an object of desire.

Fast-forward to Silicon Valley. Here, the ways ideas move is distinctive, as the social geographer Annalee Saxenian shows in her study of the contrast between the West Coast fluorescence and route 128 on the East Coast. Both regions had academic centers of excellence, but in Silicon Valley, the movement of ideas was helped by simple factors such as a better climate, a more outdoors life, and more opportunities for social interaction. In short, it promoted a different way of doing business. This more relaxed approach spread to such crucial concepts as freely sharing technological breakthroughs. In Silicon Valley, both sides were covered. From the 1950s, Stanford's Industrial Park sited next to the university campus pioneered ideas in association with industry—Hewlett Packard was one of the first companies to move in. But a short drive down the road, the building housing the Stanford Linear Accelerator was home to a bunch of free-thinking engineers who met to sound out ideas and share tips on new hardware. The Homebrew Computer Club was born out of nothing less than the pioneering spirit of Silicon Valley. Those early engineers who spotted the potential for "wonderful things" surely spent their lives bringing them out of the dark.

THE OTHER E-WORD |

> Hello. This is the earthquake information update for Thursday the
> seventh of December, 2000. 8.28 Pacific time. We have recorded
> fifteen earthquakes . . . during the last twenty-four hours.
> —U.S. Geological Survey Bay Area information line

It comes as a surprise to this outsider to learn that Silicon Valley
gets hit by earthquakes on an almost daily basis. Call up the special message line at the U.S. Geological Survey in Menlo Park and
you get the idea that the landscape, as well as everything else
around here just now, is in a constant state of flux.

The USGS at Menlo Park is the public's entry to the seismic
world. There's a seismograph printing out a trail of activity, charts
and maps and "Fancy That" facts about the causes and effects of
earthquakes. It is not a regulatory agency. "We do the science and
the state agency enacts building regulations," says USGS scientists.
In most areas there are strict seismic codes for new developments,
and properties have to be able to resist magnitude eight earthquakes. Often buildings need to be retrofitted to bring them up
to code.

The USGS seismic laboratory in Menlo Park involves up to fifty
scientists who monitor the seismic shifts by computer. Hear a

beeper go off and that's a quake registering 3.5 or more on the Richter scale. My host at the USGS in Menlo Park is Pat Jorgenson, a journalist and geographer who has been telling the story of Bay Area earthquakes for twenty years. She thinks earthquakes per se, get too much bad press. "As far as we know, no one has been killed from an earthquake in a one-storey, wood-frame home in California. Deaths come from falling masonry and multistorey structures. Earthquakes don't kill people—buildings kill people." In terms of danger to person and property, pre-1970 buildings are the biggest threat. Most of the state's historic old mission churches have been reinforced.

Fires pose a major secondary problem. In the 1906 San Francisco earthquake, after one in which the archaeologist of Troy, Heinrich Schliemann, was involved, more buildings were destroyed by fire than destroyed by the earthquake itself. Today, traffic is a serious secondary hazard. At Loma Prieta in 1989, a car-carrying freeway collapsed like a pack of cards.

In the hills above Saratoga you can see clearly see the parted landscape of the San Andreas Fault. The last quake hit the area in 1989. There are plenty of stories that come to the surface with a little judicious prompting. Businessman Max Perez was alone at his steel works in San Jose at the time of that quake. He remembers hearing a tremendous grating of metal and looking out to see waves of cars on the street. "When it subsided I went home to Cupertino to find my wife and son. They were on the lawn in a state of shock. My wife had been vacuuming and a door slammed on her hand."

The selective destruction of seismic energy meant some of their neighbors' homes were untouched. The next day Max cleared up the mess and surveyed the damage. A few cracks to the structure of the property, but the worst damage was to contents. Cabinets full of glass and china, including some treasured mementos brought back from Europe, were thrown to the ground and smashed. But such was the quixotic force of the earthquake, no windows were broken at the house.

The next day, Max shoveled the pile of shards into a trash-can. Archaeologists encountering this debris from that earthquake in some garbage heap would find evidence of a wide distribution of glass and ceramic. "Trash-can archaeology," incidentally, was pioneered by an American archaeologist, William Rathje.

Following the 1989 quake came a recession in Silicon Valley, sparked largely by changes brought about by the Gulf War. Property values slumped. Another extraordinary tale of value changes in the Valley. Such loss is intangible on the ground although anecdotal and documentary evidence, such as estate agents archives, would quantify the loss in cash figures. The lack of new building would be another clue, but such is the rate of change that, without further evidence, it is probable that changes in architectural style would be too discrete to detect.

Excavations define the strata of timescales between one historical context and the next. In general archaeology, signs of decline are marked by gaps in the record that can be "read." Indicative is the lack of upkeep of buildings or of agricultural land. Abandonment is often in line with demographic changes, the movement of populations away from certain areas. Other clues, the silting up of rivers for example, point to possible environmental causes for the downfall. Smudges of black, such as found at the site of Troy, suggest evidence of destruction by fire, catastrophes that are borne out in Homer's *Iliad* and other classical sources.

Earthquakes leave scars on the ground or tumbles of architecture. In one Roman site in the Middle East, columns the girth of redwoods are left tripped up like dominoes. Stories of earthquakes leave other traces. In China, records of earthquakes are found on ancient stelae and documents.

But back to 1989, the threatened exodus out of Silicon Valley, post quake and in recession, was clipped by the new wave of tech and the coming of the internet. Recovery was swift, developments picked up, and new buildings and businesses marked the resurgence. The population grew to meet demand with large numbers bringing their own cultures from overseas. Luxury homes, gated properties, and shopping malls with specialist stores all point to an upswing in fortunes.

The trash-can evidence would reveal the detritus of a prewired society. But if an earthquake struck today, how would the picture be different? Buildings and bridges are reinforced, but given the importance of cables and pipes—for water, sewage, not least electronic data—an earthquake would damage Silicon Valley's vital organs. And wireless technology would surely be stumped if antennae were toppled like so many columns.

Memories are short in Silicon Valley. After the most recent earthquake, people who had threatened to leave on the next ticket out became apathetic. Just now, the threat of earthquakes, rather than stories of past events, is not a subject that comes up readily in conversation. When I raise it I feel like the subject of a cartoon by the ascerbic social commentator, Bateman: the woman who mentioned "the other e-word." But at the turn of 2001, it seems there are rather more shaky economic landscapes than geological ones.

In fact, Jorgenson comments she still feels a bit cheated by the 1989 earthquake. "I was inside working at the time," she says, "I would have loved to have experienced it outside, on the ground." And feeling—and watching—the earth move at the place where its very slipperiness was being recorded must be one of those ultimate experiences that money, even in Silicon Valley, just can't buy.

THE FIFTEEN CITIES |

OK, say e-Pompeii happens. A group of archaeologists, eschewing virtual digging, decide to excavate some of Silicon Valley's mythical cities—Los Altos, Monte Sereno, Los Gatos. They dig down and find evidence of considerable wealth. Large houses with all the trappings. Digging further into the dark, rich soil they get to small dark pieces of organic matter, like stones. They get to a rough wooden box, with what appears to be writing on the top. The team gathers round as the dirt is brushed off to reveal the words—~~Saratoga Fancy Prunes~~.

Saratoga, on the mouth of a canyon, is one of Silicon Valley's golden cities. It might also have regarded itself a racy town a century ago, as much for its transforming economies as its changing names. Before its present incarnation as a discrete home for a few dot.coms, its fortunes rested in lumber, fruit farming, a thriving spa resort, vineyards, and tourism. Evidence of those changes is still visible in the landscape—along with the scar of another transforming factor in the area—the San Andreas Fault line.

Juan Bautista de Anza was the first to come through the area in 1776, but it was settled only in 1841. The settlement was named Rancho Quito by the expansive developer, Manual Alviso, who bought it in 1844. In 1848 a lumber mill was erected to provide timber for increasing numbers of settlers' homes, and a camp was founded there at a place named Campbell's Gap. In 1850 an Irish immigrant, Martin McCarty, saw a business opportunity in the making and leased the mill. Then he claimed the 230 acres of settlement, and built a toll road between the two. A paper mill and flour mill swiftly followed.

The settlement was called Toll Gate, then renamed McCartyville by its owner. In 1863, residents changed it to Bank Mills. And in 1865, a public vote changed it again to Saratoga, after the spa town in New York State. The reason for this was a matter of chemistry—the mineral waters up the canyon had a content similar to the East Coast resort. Less palatable was the origin of the Saratoga name—derived from the Indian Iroquois *se-rach-to-que,* which means "floating scum on the water."

Pacific Congress Springs became a major resort of over 720 acres, with a hotel and guest houses. It attracted hundreds of San Franciscans who came by carriage and train to escape the fog and imbibe the reputedly healing waters. The mineral water was bottled and sold around the state. An annex to the hotel was built, but in 1903 the complex burned down and was never rebuilt.

By then, Saratoga's fruit growing was quite literally blossoming. And the town had another attraction, an annual Blossom Festival, which originated in 1900 as a celebration to mark the end of a two-year drought. Better rail connections made it easy for visitors to pour into the town and the festival received worldwide acclaim. The *Saratoga Sunshine,* published by the Saratoga Improvement Association, proclaimed the town "the crown of the Valley, the Pasadena of the north." The Blossom Festival continued until 1942. By then, the agriculture economy had an added specialization. The gaps left by tree-felling in the lumber days had exposed fertile hillsides, perfect for vineyards. The Saratoga wineries continue to flourish. In 1956, Saratoga was incorporated as a city, to avoid its being subsumed in the growing San Jose.

"The orchards extended into the middle of town." Two veteran Saratogans, Hal Hodges and Willys Peck are giving me a show and tell at the Saratoga's Historical Museum as a young program-maker shoots a video of the museum for community access television. The first orchard was planted in the mid-1860s. "The land was very fertile—there was an artesian well just below the surface—so ideal for deciduous fruits. By the 1870s it was the main occupation, and by 1890s lumbering had faded out." There's a leather knee-guard used by prune pickers—"they harvested from the ground"—and special knives used to cut and remove the stone from apricots—"first they were sun dried, then treated with sulfur fumes—what hell was like, I believe." Congress Springs water bottles are highly prized. The former resort area, where locals would dig for bottles, is now inaccessible, fenced off by a water company.

Willys and his wife invite me for lunch at their home nearby. More than a pot-luck, it's a weekly "salon"; newcomers are welcomed. The old house is something of a museum in itself. Willys's father was a newspaper editor and an old printing press still functions in one of the rooms. But the pièce de résistance is the theater—not the Sensaround home entertainment center popular in the most high-tech homes, but a Greek-style theater out back. Here, the Pecks have staged numerous Shakespearean performances. The back lot also features a working locomotive and railway.

Among the other lunch guests today are Louie and Virginia Saso, who for twenty-five years cultivated one of the most comprehensive herb gardens and nurseries in America on a small plot down the road at Fruitvale Avenue. They have created a kind of herbal oasis in the midst of encroaching development, with some 1000 varieties. The gardens are watched over by a statue of St. Fiacre, the patron saint of herbs.

Their website declares: "Years ago Santa Clara Valley was alive with fruit trees, prune, apricots, cherries, pears, and more. In the spring the valley was filled with the beauty and fragrance of these blossoming trees. Most of the orchards have gone today, computers have taken over our Valley. On our little acre we are trying to show what can be done in a small area to bring back some of the beauty and fragrance that gave so much pleasure to so many in the years gone by." After their lifetime achievement, the Sasos have decided to sell the nursery. The couple is retiring over the mountains in Santa Cruz but they tell me the gardens will stay, if downsized.

Trading areas provide archaeologists with a pretty good impression of the affluence of the economy and, crucially, business networks that reach beyond the region. The main thoroughfare of Saratoga is Big Basin Way, an assortment of gourmet dining, gift shops, galleries and beauty salons. The Basin, a bar opened in 1999, prides itself on being set up in the spirit of Silicon Valley entrepreneurship. Otto Crawford, a long-time Saratogan, is one of those carefully monitoring the changes: "There is no longer a drugstore or a hardware shop." Less discernible are the unseen social changes apparent in material culture—the economic and status-conscious pulling power of places such as Saratoga. Most evenings, parking downtown is given over to the "valet" variety, such is the demand for seats in the high-end restaurants.

Big Basin Way continues up through the canyon and along the Saratoga spring through redwoods and into the mountains. It's a land of stunning views and high-end estates. The morning commutes down the twisting road and into the heart of Silicon Valley can start at 5 A.M. for the CEOs and VCs living in this area.

I stay for a few nights at one of the most desirable locations in California. Just $11 a night, for a bed in the redwood-framed Sanborn Park Hostel, on the edge of a 3,600-acre county park in the Santa Cruz Mountains. There are other great hostels in the area, but none that are plumb in the middle of Silicon Valley. The difference is apparent. On the wooden tables, the job classifieds

from the *San Jose Mercury News,* and in the evening the tap-tapping
of laptops. There is a three-night maximum stay. But some people
don't need that long. One teenager I spoke with showed up one
day with luggage, and when I next saw him at breakfast he was
checking out and moving into his own apartment. He'd just
landed a job at Apple.

All of the fifteen cities making up Silicon Valley have a pro-
nounced sense of their heritage, with active historical groups who
recognize greater significance as change accelerates. Some examples: Menlo Park has a number of historic mansions; Palo Alto's
Historical Association is housed in a significant Greek revival
building; Milpitas preserved its historic Higuera Adobe from the
1840s; Mountain View has an early pioneer cemetery. In Sunnyvale
the Iron Man Museum centers on an historic foundry, while in
Cupertino the history museum is housed in a Mediterranean-style
villa. Over in Campbell, the Tudor-style Ainsley house, and a 1921
theater are historic landmarks. A 1930s farmhouse and contents
are preserved at Los Altos. Los Gatos has a history museum inside a
preserved mill. San Jose's historic adobe building is preserved in
the shadow of the twenty-first century, the headquarters of Adobe
Software.

I speak with Carol McCarthy at her desk at Santa Clara City
Hall. Carol takes on some of the hottest challenges in Silicon Val-
ley—she is Deputy City Manager, Economic Development Team
in Santa Clara. The area has some of the biggest high-tech names—
Intel, 3COM, Yahoo!, National Semiconductor—and some of the
Valley's most historic buildings, notably the Santa Clara Mission.
Two important historical routes, the Alameda mission trail and the
El Camino Real, run from, and through, Santa Clara. The walls of
the City Hall are hung with dozens of historic photographs.

Facing Carol's office desk is a painting of an old Irish bar, Dergan's Saloon, long since gone. As a decision maker in planning and

development, but also as a Santa Clara County resident since 1980, Carol recognizes the increasing pace of change. "Everyone's more impatient." Carol and her colleagues face a tough balancing act— embracing the new development, while preserving the heritage of the city. "It's important to talk to old-timers," she says. "We're getting oral histories transcribed and trying to hold on to our past—desperately." Records, photographs, and documents are stored in acid-free boxes and handled with gloves. There are historic home tours, plaques for notable buildings, heritage trees. A donation of old magazines—one hundred boxes—was currently being inventoried. "It's a wonderful record—from farm journals to general magazines." A new Santa Clara central library will have a history room. The city also has a thriving Genealogical Society.

As we talk about the need to record the heritage of Silicon Valley, Carol takes a photograph off a wall and shows me the face of a man who remains one of her most touching links to Santa Clara's past. She reaches behind her and produces a bag, and out spill letters, photos, documents relating to the man's life, and with it Santa Clara's. Raymond R. Taylor gave Carol dozens of these artifacts over the years. After he died in 1999, his wife Mary Ellis Taylor sent Carol more of his memorabilia, together with the painting of Dergan's Bar. It turns out that not just one—but two lives were represented in the collection. Carol explains: "Ray was a close friend of James R. Bacigalupi, who owned Dergan's. 'Jimmy Batch' was twelve years on the Santa Clara City Council, six years as Mayor. Jimmy left his memorabilia to Ray, and Ray—and Mary Ellis—gave it to me for the City of Santa Clara. They all were former Santa Clara residents."

At the back of the Civic Center is the Santa Clara History Museum. It is one of the new uses for an early building, the 1913 Headen-Inman House. As with a number of historic homes in the Valley, it was moved from its original location—an achievement carried out in 1984 with the standard set of industrial rollers. It is home to the Santa Clara Arts and Historical Consortium, twenty-four local interest groups ranging from Los Fundadores—dedicated to Santa Clara's Hispanic founders—and the Mission Trail Early Ford V-8 Club. Bea Lichtenstein, who looks after the house and is writing Santa Clara's history, sees me looking into the lobby past the "closed" sign. She opens up and gives me a tour.

"Dr. Benjamin Franklin Headen and his wife, Julia, and their three children, arrived in Santa Clara in 1852, after a covered wagon trip from Rockville, Indiana . . ." Let's put that pioneering journey into Silicon Valley context. Just a century later, IBM put its first large-scale electronic computer into production. The same year it selected the city of San Jose for its first West Coast research laboratory.

Poignant reminders of the Headen family's wagon trip fill the display cases at their former home—notebooks, photographs, ephemera. Other rooms contain more aspects of Santa Clara history, the Mission churches and the arrival of the Hispanic population. There is a photograph of an early locomotive accident. And there's an elaborate wooden-framed camera. The sign says it was used for taking early twentieth-century "police mug shots." Alongside are photographs of alleged felons of diverse cultures.

It's the proverbial crisp autumn morning and I'm driving up to the hills out of Saratoga. The road goes past the familiar pattern of large new estate homes. After a while I get to the Cooper-Garrod riding stables and vineyard. It's a magnificent location. I figured that one way to touch the past in this pioneering country was to take a trail on a horse. It's an old wooden ranch, and I'm sitting on a weathered leather Western saddle that looks older than most objects I've seen in the valley for a while. I take the trail out over the ridge at a steady pace, following Susan, who used to be a high-flyer lawyer and now works with nonprofit organizations in Silicon

Early portrait of Ada Lovelace.

Valley. One day a week she comes out to ride trails. She tells me the history of the ranch. It was settled in the late nineteenth century by the Garrod family from southern England. In 1893, they bought land from the Mount Eden Orchard and Vineyard Company, and developed a thriving business. Now the sizable estate is given over to horses, and a twenty-one-acre winery. In the busy summer season, horses are brought in from Arizona.

High-tech companies bring employees out here to promote team spirit. They can probably look down and spot their headquarters in the valley stretched out below. "There's Apple, and Adobe . . ." It's indeed a rarified view. I feel a cliché spring from my lips. "It's like being back in time," I say as we trot past the remains of the fruit trees and survey the landscape contortion of an earthquake. Digging upwards for the past just for once seems to make sense.

A few days later I'm wine-tasting at a vineyard in Los Gatos. The place used to be a nunnery, now it's a winery. Three letters make a big difference. As I reach for the Cabernet Sauvignon, I notice the server's surname is "Byron." It would be too crass and too bizarre if there was a connection. So I let it drop. But the server hears my accent and tells me her husband's family "is related to Lord Byron. . . ." Dennis Byron comes over and I tell him I've just been writing about one of the family, Ada Lovelace. Standing in the heart of Silicon Valley with a barful of techies, I'm not sure who's more fazed by this nth degree of separation.

I REMEMBER THE ORCHARDS . . . |

Fruit orchards and canning plants were economic mainstays, and many
people came of age picking fruit in orchards.
—*Silicon Valley 2010,* on agricultural heritage

Ask around in the older businesses and homes of Silicon Valley,
and there will likely be to hand one or two faded color photographs of the "Valley of Heart's Delight." It's also the name of
a film made in the 1920s, which perfectly captures the spirit
of the time. Most of the local libraries have a copy of it, and it's
well worth viewing as a social documentary that shows not only
the way things looked back then, but the way people felt about
their relationship to work. After a week picking fruit, pitting it,
packing it, and hauling it—what better than to spend Sunday
at rest?

Farm workers would plan outings. They'd relish a few idle
hours in the beauty spots around the Santa Clara Valley. Those who
had transport would delight in the drive out to places like Castle
Rock. And there they would just bask in the view out to the Santa
Cruz Mountains. No fruit trees around to return their thoughts to
work. Just a picnic spread and a whole day for play.

After a few weeks driving the freeways, I put out a call to my source of all things computer historical, Sellam Ismail, of the Vintage Computer Festival. Do you know of any orchards? I get a batch of emails in reply.

> Are there any original orchards left in the Silicon Valley?

They just tore down that Olson (cherry I think) orchard next to their stand, but I believe there is still a small orchard across the street. Have her look in Morgan Hill or Gilroy. Remember, at one time all these south bay cities were separated by open space like a drive down Monterey highway.
—Doug

Los Altos, on the east side of San Antonio Road and toward the north side of the downtown area. But it's more of a historical exhibit than a real orchard. She may also want to check out the Los Altos History House in that same area.
—Frank McConnell

They are getting harder to find, there is a part of the old cherry orchard left on Mathilda by the Sunnyvale Tennis center. If the plum orchard is the one I think it is, then it succumbed earlier this year.
—Chuck

There's a small farm where there used to be an orchard on the corner of Levin and Grant in Mountain View. . . .
—Joe

At a book reading in Berkeley, I find I'm sitting next to a man whose friend has an orchard, though I don't quite know how the conversation got there from Alain de Botton's *Consolations of Philos-*

ophy. Anyway, the man says he'd be glad to put us in touch. I arrange to go to see the friend in Santa Clara.

Not sure what to expect, this being my first assigned Silicon Valley orchard, I am looking for a forest of green. The address checks out to a residential area and a modest house. A smiling Bruce Roberts welcomes me and we go out to see the orchard in his back lot. There are six trees. And Bruce can name them all. "This is an olive tree, it predates the house . . . it's about 100 years old. This is a quince tree. And a lemon-orange grafted tree. A fig tree. An almond. And a lemon tree." There is also a grapevine.

The house was built by a Portuguese man on land that used to be owned by the Catholic church. Bruce, who tells me he works for a start-up, has planted a variety of vegetables and fruits—strawberries, cherry tomatoes, lettuce, broccoli, celery, lima beans, beets, and peas. He says tending the soil is a great way to unwind after a day of tech.

He offers me a fruit from the lemon-orange tree. It's a novelty to me. Another new thing in Silicon Valley.

Bruce Roberts, Silicon Valley, May 2000.

The "orchard issue" hangs over me like an apple bough for the next few weeks, as I try to pin down a larger place with a history and a story to tell. I drive past construction sites where orchards used to be, and see countless photographs of the way the landscape looked when trees crowded the horizon of the Santa Clara Valley.

I figure C. J. Olson's in Sunnyvale is the place. The cherry orchard on El Camino and Mathilda Avenue is part of local folklore, as much for its latest chapter as its historic past. A banner proclaims Olson's web address but at the front is an old-style fruit stand, baskets brimming ruby red.

In 1999, the orchard celebrated its centenary year. But it also marked a big change, as a vast part of the acreage was sold off to developers. It was a bittersweet move that shook up the Olson family farm, one of the few left in the valley. The attendant publicity also raised the then largely unspoken issue of how much development is enough in Silicon Valley.

I go to see Deborah Olson, the latest generation of her family to take over the business. She is one of the cheeriest people I encounter in my travels in the valley. It turns out she is a world authority on cherries and she travels to see orchards and growers all over the globe. In a couple of days she's heading for Chile. "Cherries are my passion." And not only her passion it seems—there's even an "unofficial" cherry lovers' site on the internet.

The name Olson has been synonymous with cherries in the Santa Clara Valley for four generations. And Deborah's more than a successful businesswoman, she's an evangelist for the fruit. When we meet she's wearing a sweater embroidered with a bunch of cherries. Her office at the back of the fruit stand has a cherry motif at every turn, right down to the red speckled rug. From this modest business space, the Olson's cherry empire sends its produce worldwide. The company has even supplied the doyen of American living, Martha Stewart.

The orchard was planted by Carl and Hannah Olson at the end of the nineteenth century. They came to the United States as immigrants from Sweden. The orchard began as five acres purchased for $750, that's $150 an acre. A century later, land there is worth from $1 million to $5 million an acre.

Deborah used to walk to work through a forest of cherry trees. The Olson orchards spread over thirty acres. Her home, and those of other members of the family, was set in the midst of them. And from childhood to adulthood, Deborah's life was marked by the cycles of spring growth, pink blossom, first fruits, harvest, and winter replenishment.

After years of working with fruit on the farm—picking, pitting, and selling—Deborah took a college degree in food and nutrition. And then she spent eight years in France as an apprentice to several top chefs. It was a shrewd move. Back in California, Deborah applied her skills back at the fruit stand, devising new Olson's products such as fruit and cherry blossom honey. More than marketing, it was a way of ensuring the company's survival as new factors began to bite—unseasonal weather, increased agricultural regulations concerning irrigation and spraying.

Then things changed rapidly. The trees were not producing fruit; some were dying of a root disease. And the Santa Clara Valley was changing. Orchards were losing out to the demands of tech in more ways than land use. The labor pool was drained of agricultural workers as the original harvest workers were growing old. It would seem a logical time to do what so many others had done. Sell off all the land and retire someplace else. And that's what some members of the Olsen family wanted to do. But not Deborah or her father, Charles. There was a lawsuit and, eventually, a compromise. Seventeen acres were sold off to developers.

On Labor Day, 1999, when Deborah and her father were away on vacation, bulldozers moved in and felled 1000 trees. There was a lightning storm. A year later, and Deborah is still visibly moved by the memory. "I cried, I was depressed." She received a shoal of emails of support and witnessed an unleashed emotion not usually associated with the hard-edge of Silicon Valley.

"People grieved as the felling day approached," she said. "They said they felt helpless." But Deborah, not one to let her spirits drop, countered the loss with a celebration in the orchard. She held a series of parties for the old cherry pickers going back fifty years. Some of them had stories to tell about her grandparents. It was a catharsis. "A way of moving forward," she said. "Hearing people talk about the orchards as they were provides a continuum for the future." The fruit stand stays as a landmark and a tribute to another way of life.

The new development is nearly completed. It is a mixed-use complex, with residential and retail buildings. Apartments will house scores of workers and their families. Many will be from the high-tech companies. Once the decision was made to sell the land, Deborah remained unflappably involved. "I interviewed around thirty developers over two years. It was an education," she says of her dealings, as a single female, with predominantly male developers.

The new complex looks out over the remaining fifteen acres of orchards. The cherry heritage is retained in the name of the development—and in the interior design. The luxury clubhouse will feature fabrics festooned with cherries—Deborah's hand of course.

But from the simplicity of a single grower comes the complexity of market demands and availability. The Olsons keep their hands in the soil by raising a small cherry harvest, and also apricots. The fruit stand continues to be stocked with their fruit, and produce from local farmers. Other growers' cherries shipped in from Chile will help to meet demand from long-established customers. Eight years ago Deborah introduced a mail-order catalog.

Deborah still lives in the same house, but the walk to work is through a childhood landscape that has changed for good. "My great-grandparents' house is gone," she says, suddenly collecting herself. "It's still tough. It's a challenge."

As I'm listening to Deborah's story, at the back of my mind is Anton Chekhov's play, *The Cherry Orchard.* It's also about a family accommodating to change over time and the pressure of development. The setting is Russia at the turn of the twentieth century. The family's cherry orchard is finally felled. The last sound the audience hears is the steady chop-chop of an ax.

HOW ARTY IS MY VALLEY? |

Enter Hotspur, reading a letter.

Hotspur: How now Kate! I must leave you within these two hours.
Lady Percy: O my good lord, why are you thus alone?
For what offence have I this fortnight been
A banish'd woman from my Harry's bed?
Tell me, sweet lord, what is't that takes from thee,
Thy stomach, pleasure and thy golden sleep?
Why dost thou bend thine eyes upon the earth,
And start so often when thou sit'st alone?
Why hast thou lost the fresh blood in thy cheeks . . . ?
—*Henry IV,* part, I

August 2000, Cupertino. Free Shakespeare in the Park, part of the San Francisco Shakespeare Festival. The stage direction for Hotspur's entrance is apparently amended for this tech-sponsored event: "Enter Hotspur, reading an email from a laptop." The audience gets it.

Think of the relationship between visual art and Silicon Valley and the image is invariably digital. It's perhaps hardly surprising that the creative minds that developed machines and software also push the boundaries in graphics, animation, and other techniques that were once hand-drawn and are now keyboarded. Earlier, landscapes, symbols, and portraits emerged out of computer code print-outs. Sellam Ismail has a great example as part of his collection—a vast airplane "drawn" in code—zeros and ones—heads out over the Golden Gate Bridge. Programmer/artist unknown.

Whether the practice of computer programming is an art is the stuff of mixed opinions. Jim Warren, the West Coast Computer Fayre pioneer, reckons it is intrinsically all the same. "Many of the talents necessary in art, in any creative activity, are equally essential in programming." Jim, whose roots lie in the arts and ideas fusion of 1970s technology, goes on: "In programming you have to see something that doesn't exist, how its parts interrelate." Elsewhere, though, my proposition to explore the art of this tech landscape was greeted with derision—"Art? In Silicon Valley?'

The distinctive towers of the Adobe Software building in San Jose play on the city's historic architecture. It's close by another adobe, the historic Mission building on the tourist trail. My particular trail for this interview started in Las Vegas, at a digital photography show. I saw Julieanne Kost's engaging Photoshop™ presentation, and I thought of archaeology.

It's a point not lost on the artist. Described officially as an Adobe Evangelist, Julieanne works out of a cubicle, the workspace characteristic of Silicon Valley. She paints with layers of images, piling them up, stripping them back—partially, fully, adding again. What she ends up with is distinctive and beautiful, and in a manner of its process, archaeological. Collages using numerous and seemingly disparate visual cues work together and create this digital "art." The technology allows each of Julieanne's movements to be recorded in an archive. There is a history of her palette. She can go back to older images—back in creative time—and recall how she achieved effects, and how the layers of color and texture and meaning come together to describe her abstract impressions. "I am not looking for the perfect photo," she says, "but anything that causes an emotional reaction. I don't know what I am working toward. Something will just appear. I will know that images work together, but I won't know why."

Julieanne takes me through an image—"Surgery Flat"—created using Adobe Photoshop™. It is a multiplicity of layers—tractor tread, moss, a women's back—actually Julieanne's to represent her mother's immobilized vertebrae—more organic material, sand dollars. The component parts are played with, teased, softened, textured until the artist is satisfied. Being digital, the image can be stored and restored over time. Julieanne's art is intangible in creation, but tangible in its quality as an artifact. She exhibits the digital images as prints in galleries, 16 × 16 inches.

Visual art goes further than the digital kind in this environment. I found public sculptures inspired by images of new technology, such as one near the entrance to Stanford University. And there are private artworks commissioned by those who have made their fortunes in Silicon Valley. The walls of many of the multimillion-dollar homes are filled with artworks where those who do not collect computers, collect more traditional artifacts. Corporations lease artworks or have something designed that reflects their product. One example grabs attention in the lobby of a computer part recycler in San Jose. It's a collage made entirely of pieces of integrated circuits, motherboards, pieces of gold, copper worked like lace and, in a surprising twist, feathers.

And throughout the fifteen cities, there are traditional art groups, meeting as they have done for decades. There are classes and workshops, where the ranks may be swelled by a few tech workers rediscovering the traditional art forms of still-life and nudes, watercolor painting, pottery, calligraphy, and printmaking. And then there is the art of Silicon Valley that springs out of the multifarious cultures, from the precision of Japanese wood-blocks to the aesthetics of Indian carvings.

What I looked for but didn't find in this search was a new industrial art that reflected the culture of the Valley in the way the early days of railways or electricity were captured by artists of the time. I longed to see the work of the new generation of Edward Hoppers setting up easels in Santa Clara County. They would be painting moodily lit cyberscapes, cafes where the tables are heavy with laptops, or the strips of El Camino where generations of signs peel and pulsate. The titles would hint at the culture of Silicon Valley. Some examples: "Infinite Loop, Fall"; "Waiting for the VTR, First Street, San Jose"; "Chinese Lunch, Mountain View"; "Rush Hour, 4 P.M., Route 101"; "Cubicle, Midnight, Cupertino." In Los Angeles, I came close. A young artist had set up his easel on the sidewalk opposite a vast Apple computer ad that featured Charlie Chaplin. He was painting that image as it appeared as part of the cityscape.

"Can you see it yet?" A balmy summer evening, and I am walking toward the front entrance of the Westin Hotel in Palo Alto. The first new hotel in Palo Alto for fifteen years. Using a borrowed cellphone, I am getting directions to a sculpture. This could be a new type of performance art. In fact, after driving past the area numerous times in traffic without my spotting his vast monumental artwork, sculptor David Middlebrook is taking no chances.

So, round the corner, face the lobby and—"Yes, I see it!" It is blatantly archaeological in its inspiration, but contemporary in concept. The sculpture draws on several themes from the past. Old World megaliths—giant standing stones—reach for the sky and reveal an underside based on Lascaux cave paintings from France. This is topped off, quite literally, with a symbolic representation of molecular structure—ergo the science at the heart of Silicon Valley technology. The stone base is volcanic basalt from the Cascade mountains in the northern United States. The cave paintings are incised, colored, and polished. At night they are illuminated and glow as if reflecting firelight.

A few minutes out of Los Gatos, Middlebrook's sculpture studio nestles in a verdant nature setting, between creek and road. In this suitably inspirational workplace, he produces significant public works and private commissions for individuals and corporations. The amiable Middlebrook also heads up the renowned art department at San Jose State University.

His huge studio is the kind of space I had forgotten existed in Silicon Valley. It is luxurious with work surfaces piled with stuff. The walls house photographs and visual scraps. There is a sense of creative disorder. Or orderly chaos. Outside, pieces of maquette and works-in-progress decorate the yard in an ad hoc manner.

Middlebrook's assistant is fine tuning a new piece for a local collector. Against the heat and smell of metalworking, Middlebrook tells me about the passion behind his design for the Westin sculpture. "I've always been interested in forgotten people, in outsiders, the ancient tribes, native American Indians. This sculpture is at the core of my being. I was thinking about how quickly the United States has downplayed the integrity of primal cultures." Working on the sculpture was an intense experience. At his studio, he projected transparencies of the Lascaux paintings onto the basalt, and played around with the shapes and textures. "I was virtually in a trance. I was imagining myself as a caveman . . ."

Middlebrook shows me the model he constructed, one of a number put up by sculptors who submitted for the commission. He tells me the hotel was not even built at the time. He used the architect's plans and painted the building as he thought it should look. In the end the finished sculpture sits outside a hotel painted just like the model.

And so, a public artwork inspired by early technologies of stone shaping and cave painting ends up close to the entrance to Stanford University, at the heart of Silicon Valley's tech boom, standing outside the lobby of a hotel built to service the effect of that transformation.

There's another interesting melding of arts and science out toward Half Moon Bay on the Pacific coast. Caltrans, California's highways authority, worked with an artist to create a "rock art" effect on a new wall on the freeway.

Probably unnoticed by most drivers, the newly constructed wall sits as part of the landscape. Its reinforced concrete appearance has given way to striations and daubs in rusts, sandy, earthy colors. It's a treatment to blend in the face of the retaining wall. So convincing is it on first sighting that I am knee-jerked into looking for the marks left by prehistoric rock artists. Lyle Oehler, at Caltrans, tells me the effect was devised with the aid of a specialist in concrete forming who happened to hold a fine arts degree. It helped that he was also a rock climber. A team of semiskilled staff spray-painted the concrete. In time vegetation will add to the new tech landscape of the highway wall.

Silicon Valley's main art space is in downtown San Jose. The Museum of Modern Art, near the Tech and the Convention Center, holds exhibitions that complement its high-tech and design-enamored setting. A collaboration with the Whitney in New York considered American art in the age of technology. The San Jose MOMA is housed at the Plaza de Cezar Chavez. It is a site that features a nineteenth-century post office, serving as a café, and the new modern addition, which holds its main exhibition space. Also downtown, the San Jose Institute of Contemporary Art is concerned with the work of Silicon Valley's newest artists, while WORKS/San Jose celebrates experimental and multimedia approaches.

San Jose might have had another major gallery when Myles O'Connor, who made his fortune from gold, offered his collection of paintings and sculptures to the city. The money was raised to build a gallery to house the collection, but was used instead for a statue of President McKinley after he was assassinated. O'Connor and his wife gave their collection to an institution in Washington, D.C. instead.

Arts Council Silicon Valley is a nonprofit organization that distributed more than $4 million to benefit the arts between 1991 and 1999. The money has gone to arts organizations, artists, schools, community groups, and social services agencies. The funding comes from a variety of sources—from arts foundations to corporations. These include the William and Flora Hewlett Foundation, the David and Lucile Packard Foundation, Lockheed Martin Missiles and Space, and the Luke B. Hancock Foundation. The ArtsChoice workplace-giving campaign also draws contributions from SiVa workers, including employees for Adobe Systems, Applied Materials Inc., Cirrus Logic, and a number of Silicon Valley city councils, state bodies, UCSF/Stanford Health Care, and Stanford University. And individuals and families give through the Santa Clara County voluntary property tax campaign.

"Silicon Valley's phenomenal economic growth is fueling growth in the arts but largely in an indirect way—such as audiences growing, museum attendance up; the percentage of contribution is up, but not in proportion to wealth." Bruce Davis heads up the Silicon Valley Arts Council and I'm talking to him about the oft-quoted idea that there is a Renaissance going on. "No, there's public art and an exponential rise in cultural activities, but it's not quite an artistic renaissance." Although there is some patronage of the arts, inasmuch as wealthy dot.comers are commissioning works for their new homes, the e-conomy has led to major artistic displacements in San Francisco.

However, the tech-initiated cultural mix provides a considerable boost for the arts in the public eye. Throughout the year, festivals are a growing part of the Silicon Valley scene. "There's no better way to reflect diversity," says Davis.

A look down the list of organizations funded in 1999 reveals a broad spectrum of cultures. Some examples: the Kaishan of San Jose Dance Company (Filipino); Los Lupenos (Latino); Oriki Theatre (African); Chinese Performing Artists of America; Arte Flamenco de San Jose; Association for Viet Arts; Abhinaya Dance Company of San Jose (India); Mostly Irish Theater Company; Polynesian Cultural Association; Pusaka Sunda (West Java); Xipe Totec (Aztec); Yi Ai Kai (Japanese American); Grupo Folclorico Tempos de Outrora (Portugese); Arab Women's Solidarity Association; and the Arts and Cultural Society of San Jose (for Iranian dance and music).

There are cultural collaborations—Ensemble International produced a concert of folk dances of Poland, Russia, Austria, and America—and community programs such as the Arts Program at Stanford Hospital, which provides artists' venues, entertainment, and classes.

A number of major companies sponsor cultural events such as free open air theater and music festivals, a form of promotional philanthropy. With such a wealth hub in the area, the SiVa Arts Council continually looks for ways to get corporations involved in arts funding. But it's not an easy task. A few corporations operate a "no arts funding" policy. "It's often an arts versus science dichotomy. This is a valley of engineers. Although creativity and innovation seem to be the hallmark of Silicon Valley, this goes into products for consumption," says Bruce Davis. The feeling is that there is simply no time to produce "art for art's sake."

Over in Palo Alto, the cultural mix includes a thriving Arts Center, and the Landmark, a historic cinema restored to architectural splendor thanks to a high-tech benefactor, the Packard Foundation. Stanford itself has the art and artifacts of the Iris and Gerald B. Cantor Arts Center and a garden that features one of the largest collections of Rodin sculptures outside France.

Just off the main drag of University Avenue, the Pacific Art League of Palo Alto was founded in 1921 as an arts club. The first members of this institution were artists and from the upper social classes. It had connections with Stanford University and the presidential Hoover family. Over time, it became more democratic and community-centric. It is now run as a nonprofit organization. Its current membership is made up from Palo Alto, Santa Clara, and San Mateo County. The development of Palo Alto as one of the hubs of Silicon Valley is not lost on The Pacific Art League. The making, buying, or viewing of art is marketed as an alternative to the pace of life in the Valley. As part of an initiative called "Artists at Work," it has a tie up with another organization, Bootstrap, to place a number of artists in Silicon Valley companies. The idea is that a company will sponsor an artist for a full week of work. In return for space, the artist will produce art that is "local" to the scene. The brochure describes: "We expect this synergism to give rise to a unique expression of Silicon Valley at the opening of the twenty-first century."

Joe Hardegree at Pacific Art tells me: "The idea is to expose the artists to workers, to the culture of Silicon Valley." So Edward Hoppers might come out of it? "We would expect to see a reflection of valley life in the results." But he adds another consideration that perhaps the most desirable artworks would deliberately not draw on the artifacts or reflect the pace of daily life. "People don't want to replicate their workspace."

The Triton Gallery, close by the sculpture-flanked civic center in Santa Clara, is a space that celebrates the Valley's cultural diversity. Wandering round the exhibits, I'm drawn to an image of an ancient Egyptian site, created by the Berkeley artist Robert Z. Apte. This image purports to be "The true Abu Simbel, 1998." Given that this site was flooded by the construction of the Aswan dam by then, I am intrigued by this feat of imagination. I look closer. The image is a digital photograph, worked over and montaged. Apte elaborates on the idea of using technology to manipulate the image, "and therefore the viewer." By taking an ancient site that is lost to public gaze, and offering a lost view of it, Apte is artist as archaeologist. And best of all, the digital image of ancient Egypt is printed on papyrus.

Digital art moves from paper to textile. A woman in Saratoga showed me a quilt she had made from a patchwork of family photos. She had them scanned onto cotton fabric at her local Kinko's Copy Shop. At the Webby Awards in San Francisco—the Oscars of cyberworld—one guest reportedly flaunted her NewCentury-School-Book.com site in a wrap made from an iron-on transfer of her webpage.

SIGNS AND SYMBOLS |

September, 2000. Heading north out of Silicon Valley at San Francisco, there's a motel sign. Neon-lit. The sort of feature that fits snugly in the contemporary landscape of America as part of the drive culture. Except this is no real motel sign, it's a pastiche, an advertisement for one of the successes of the internet age—Yahoo!.com.

In this colossal road-side image, postbomb and postmodern stand together between the iconic "Golden Gate" and the "Valley of Heart's Delight." The route links the world of Haight-Ashbury and the free-enterprising days of early computer technology with the New Age of Silicon Valley and the dot.com entrepreneurs. And it's the whippet-slick cyber heroes who will smile at the irony of the sign as they wait in the growing queues on the freeway.

When I first saw that billboard in January 2000, it seemed the perfect way to launch a discussion of old and new material culture. It was a recycling of a concept, a smart repackaging of something so quintessentially American, and yet one involved with a truly global product, accessible in most parts of the world.

In 1996, Yahoo! was one of the first internet sites to use television advertising. It made something tangible from a virtual brand.

It was an advertisement about fishing. A simple concept—having no luck, why not search using bait?

The lobby of Yahoo! in Santa Clara. It's the same gourmet coffee, fresh fruit, glossy magazine working environment that has come to typify the successful Silicon Valley company. The lobby color scheme is purple and yellow, the company's distinctive logo is a custom made typeface. The lobby has a display of Yahoo! goods—hats, tee-shirts, and so on, in a glass cabinet. They could be goods in a hotel shop, or artifacts in a museum. The space also features a large model bovine from New York City's annual Cow Parade. It is being equipped with a computer so passers-by can check their email.

On the lobby tables are photo albums. They are filled with happy snaps of Yahoo! employees having fun. Glenn Tokunaga, Yahoo!'s art director, insists: "We're very conservative for an Internet company, but we try to be fun." Ideas for marketing come from anywhere in the company—"the great things is we can implement ideas quickly." What had undoubtedly helped Yahoo!'s growth was that the cheeky catchphrase—the question "Do you Yahoo!?"—has entered colloquial language.

I'm at Yahoo! to get a fuller picture on the billboard from Karen Edwards, in the marketing department. The company had set out to create a landmark with the motel signs, erected in San Francisco and New York in 1998. The designers, Blackrock, shrewdly realized the market audience would respond to the historically retro graphic, while latching on to the highly contemporary product. A product that was not even a tangible "thing" that could be picked off the shelf, but an e-thing, as electronically generated as neon lights around the billboard.

Over a short time, the sign has become part of the landscape of New York City, as it has on the highway in San Francisco. Not only is the sign a great marketing success, it has taken on a life of its own. It's such a landmark in New York City that wedding couples get pictured with it.

As the company's services had expanded, Edwards explains, the company's marketing had been reshaped to accommodate and make the site a place to stay. The motel concept is more than a neat design. It has a subtext that represents the company's way of marketing itself as "not just a place you go to find things, but a home away from home, where you feel comfortable." Occasionally, the "motel" sign's wording changes, reinforcing the site as a destination with such incentives as "waterbeds."

The cost of the billboard was significant. "It was more important to make a large investment in a high profile area than spending the same on something more transitional," says Edwards. There's another version for Japan. "We aim to represent something fun and friendly, but not too quirky."

The "motel" version in Manhattan is less techie in design, more fitting for a place with a Silicon Alley than a Valley. It's also a more accessible sign. Members of the public, techie or not, are part of the process of cultural transformation. "People meet by the sign, have their pictures taken under it—and then send us the photos!" says Edwards. Thus the sign becomes a cultural landmark. It's associated with New York memories and, in this way, the chain can be seen that relates people, to place, to thing. The sign has even hosted a marriage proposal.

I'm driving down a stretch of El Camino Real, the Royal Road, a trail first trodden out of the landscape by the ancient Ohlone. It was the main route for stage coaches between San Jose and Monterey on the Pacific coast. Today its flashcard of signs signal the recent changes. The businesses are a mix of old and established and young and thrusting. The signs are all points in between. There are faded paint, day-glo neon, illuminated plastic, stick-on letters, digital displays. On soaring poles perched over the road, and at poke-you-in-the-eye-level. There are blocks of themes. Runs of restaurants—Vietnamese, traditional American diners, fast-food Korean, sushi houses. Signs for one-man bands, banks of account- ants, tire chains, and tech companies. Signs for generic shopping malls. Fluttering emblems of flag-waving car dealers, with their three-figure, four-figure, and high-end stock. Signs for pull-ins, drive-ins, and the shuttered light of liquor stores. "See's Candy" where the little old lady beams a sweet smile of nostalgia. And right across from this on El Camino, a tattooist's banner for "The House of Pain."

San Jose's Tech Museum has innovation quite literally written into its foundation. The words of some of Silicon Valley's leading innovators, Gordon Moore and Robert Noyce, are inscribed into the fabric of the buildings. Etched in stone, like a series of Roman inscriptions.

I'm musing over this when Sellam sends me something inter- esting. Well, pretty unintelligible to me, but interesting. It's part of a coding print out—and some of its content is in Latin. Neither of us reads Latin, and I don't read code—so it's, well, doubly Greek to me. I send a copy to a neo-Luddite classicist friend at Oxford University.

```
... ***************************************************
;;;
... * *
;;;
... * *
;;;
;;; * Copyright (c) 1978 by Massachusetts Institute of *
;;;; * Technology and Honeywell Information Systems, Inc. *
... * *
;;;
;;; * *
;;;
... ***************************************************
;;;
...
;;;
...
;;;
;;;      Multics EMACS Redisplay
```

;;;   Greenberg, March 1978

;;;   3/6/78 inceptus Luna meo adjutorio.

;;;   4/19/78 duas fenestras feci.

;;;   5/30/78 ^V creavi.

;;;   6/18/78 signum linearum elongatarum, ^0^L, &c

;;;   7/5/78 Cuncta lineae comparandae sunt, quicumque sint.

;;;   7/27/78 Ostendae sunt lineae quae non in textu sunt.

;;;   8/23/78 Dua fenestrae tacebant, atque mundae factae erant.

;;;   9/6/78 Indices linearum originalum per fenestris comparo.

;;;   3/1/79 Quando laboro in medio linearum elongatarum, omnes
moveatur.

;;;   4/4/79 Minibuffer in multos divisus est.

;;;   4/12/79 Mille fenestrae florent.

;;;   8/24/79 ^V et ESC-V argumentes dedi.

;;;   Septembri 1979 hoc redisplicator Paltere sustenetur.

;;;   2/12/80 tty-no-cleolp impletur,

;;;   mode-line-hook & local-display-end-string

;;;   10/23/80 Praefix minibufferis non delendum est.

;;; 1980 Decembri e manibus meis dimissi te ut sole per mundum
ambules.

;;;

Sellam does a quick excavation of the data. "This program is responsible for redrawing the screen display in EMACS, a text-
editing program that is popular among hardcore hackers in the
Unix world."

He picks out some familiar words among the Latin—
"minibuffer and some Unix code identifiers such as tty-no-cleopl,
mode-line-hook, etc. And 'fenestras' is I believe 'window' so it's
probably referring to the screen display."

While the next three lines of the data make sense to the non
techie –Homer creeps in with "rosy-fingered dawn" from the
Odyssey—

```
;;; Welcome to the rosy-fingered dawn of the New Era:
;;;       Presenting, at popular demand;
;;;       A Comment In English!
;;;
```

Even Sellam is baffled by the following section. "These comments are too cryptic. I guess they were only meant to be understood by the programmers actually working on the code."

```
;;;       30 June 1981 Extending local displays, Richard Mark Soley
;;;       1 July 1981 suppress-remarks and minibuffer-clear-all, Richard
Soley
;;;       5 November 1981 truncate overlength modelines, Richard Soley
;;;       19 August 1982 fixed inverse-real-world-xcoord for \c lines,
;;;                       Barry Margolin
;;;       20 August 1982 added CAH's real underlining code, Barry
Margolin
;;;       12 October 1982 modified underlining to use constant 400,
Barmar
;;;
```

Signs in public places in Silicon Valley, such as on buses, are written in three languages—American English, Spanish, and Vietnamese. Street names are in the first two, reflecting the earlier history of the place. The next addition indicates a new history, the high-tech heritage. Woz Way in San Jose is named after Steve Wozniak of Apple. And then there are addresses on old roads that say something new. Their cachet comes from their location on the stretches around Santa Clara, Cupertino, and Mountain View, which are home to household names or have early tech connections. The Sand Hill Road near Atherton, for venture capitalists, the sign announcing the Stanford Linear Accelerator, for memories of the "Homebrew Club." Any "Fry's" sign for a slice of geek heaven.

Tech enthusiasts think in code, write in code—and to the un-trained ear, speak in code, with a language string of letters and numbers. In 1996, two editors of the tech-vogue magazine, *Wired,* gave the nontechie a leg up with *Wired Style,* described as "A *Chicago Manual of Style* for the millennium" by *Newsweek* magazine. The book's subtitle is "Principles of English Usage in the Digital Age." Authors and geekspeak experts, Jessie Scanlon and Connie Hale, reach from Abilene Project—"a high-speed backbone for advanced technologies"—to zine "a small, cheap, self-published work," via drag and drop, MorF, TED, and thread.

Uses and abuses are cited. For example, ROM. "Don't spell out read-only memory; do pronounce it 'rahm.'"

And it makes the most of the conversion of visual gags into acronyms. ROTFL is "online shorthand for rolling on the floor laughing." The writers add: "more energetic than ROTF (rolling on the floor)."

The speed of change forces a new way of communicating: "Think blunt bursts and sentence fragments. Writing that is on-the-fly—even frantic," suggest the authors in the first of their ten "principles for writing well in the digital age."

I meet Jessie at the *Wired* office in downtown San Francisco. It's a great opportunity to gawp at the home of the digerati's style magazine. Its bright pink door does not disappoint.

"We watch language at play," says Jessie. "We dig into etymologies. We're excited and obsessed by the evolution of language, and how that reflects shifts in our culture." The wired culture is the global village and the new media. Wired words come off the street or from the lab. The pace is fast. The message reflects the medium or—zap!—is keystroked into etherdust, or "vaporware" as the authors would have it. *Wired* style is addictive.

Netiquette is an evolving concept. Email is "as fast as a telegram and as cheap as a whisper." There is a paradox of ethereal formality. Free-floating electrons netted by parameters.

As Dr. Johnson or Webster would no doubt agree, one process is crucial to the lexicon. Inclusion or exclusion? "When a new technical term, a bullshit buzzword, or an especially gnarly acronym hits our screens, we send emails to various editors and style divas." Word watchers include Eric S. Raymond, author of *The New Hacker's Dictionary* and its associated online jargon file. Other times, and more prosaically, Scanlon and Hale use "gut-instinct."

In 1999, *"Wired Style"* was updated and revised from its first version. Cue change-over-time—three years is an age in the cyberworld. And this is now the age of e-commerce. World Wide Web and internet-related words lace the revision. "Language seems to be in a period of high-speed evolution. Just look at how quickly the prefix of the moment changes," says Jessie. "Net, cyber, web, I, e—even the Ehype is passing by already. . . ."

Other signs and wonders inhabit Silicon Valley. Drive around the cities for long enough and you'll surely come across a spiritual medium, advertising loudly on a banner—"Tarot," "Palm Reading," or just plain "Psychic."

One of America's top-selling spiritualists, Sylvia Browne, is based in Campbell. I didn't manage to interview this busy lady. But I did have one unexpected spiritual encounter. Chasing up the story of Larry Ellison's "Japanese" styled home in Woodside, I rang directory assistance for the number of the headquarters of this software giant. Got the number. Dialed it. Female voice replied with sound of TV in background. I ask for Larry Ellison's office. "You've got the wrong number." "Sorry. I thought this was Oracle." "It is Oracle." "Oh." "Oracle Soul Searching. You want a psychic?"

SIVA—THE CONCEPT |

Silicon Valley seems to be the one that has gotten exactly right the intricate combination of infrastructure, climate, universities, venture capital, lifestyle, megasuccess stories, major research institutions, and risk-taking business attitude.

—Californian travel writer Martin Cheek on tech centers worldwide, in the *Silicon Valley Handbook*

Leonard Hoops is marketing master of all he surveys. From his office high above San Jose, he looks out over the sprawling cityscape with a smile of satisfaction. San Jose is the capital of Silicon Valley. And Silicon Valley is the undisputed tech capital of the world.

Hoops is vice-president of the San Jose Visitors' Bureau and Convention Center. And in the midst of all the high-tech hype, he also has the task of persuading the public that it's not all tech-talk in the Valley. There's more to the city than that.

But let's start with the main reason people have heard of Silicon Valley. "Yes, it's the real tomorrow land!" Hoops is incurably enthusiastic—with good cause. The products he has to sell would be highly marketable even without the SiVa factor. The keynote Tech Museum of Innovation. The Children's Discovery Museum. The

Pacific Coast, near Silicon Valley, January 2000.

significant San Jose Museum of Modern Art. The Convention Center. The Hispanic heritage and Peralta adobe. Add such attractions as the sports—the San Jose Arena, home of the Sharks—the performing arts, fun parks such as Paramount's Great America, and the architectural landmarks—the Winchester Mystery House, the Rosicrucian Egyptian Museum, the Lick Observatory on Mount Hamilton. And then tie this in with the B.S.V.—Before Silicon Valley—historical backbone. After all, San Jose was the first city settled in California, and dates from 1777. And in a curious process of accidental archaeology, the digging of trenches to lay cables for technology-hungry Silicon Valley has revealed a series of particularly sensitive find sites. These are the burial places used by significantly earlier inhabitants, the Native Americans.

Hoops knows that computer enthusiasts have no trouble finding a reason to visit San Jose, to base themselves in a wired hotel room, and take a bus tour around the garages, cubicles, and monumental architecture of new technology history.

The problem comes when people think that's all there is to San Jose and its environs. The Silicon Valley branding has to encompass the material past and the intangibilities of the cutting-edge future. There is nowhere on earth quite like it. My own enthusing over the place comes as some surprise to Hoops. It's not been easy convincing the international press, for example, that San Jose is the gateway to things other than geek heaven. The city is the eleventh largest in the United States. It's bigger than San Francisco, which comes as a revelation. In the course of its redevelopment it's rediscovering its heritage and holding on to it tight. The bill for the new city hall is upped by millions of dollars to allow the moving of a small, but significant, number of historic buildings.

I tell Hoops about the discoveries I've made along the way, when I wore my tourist hat for a long weekend. A base in San Jose opened up a different part of northern California—one that reaches down to the Pacific Ocean at Half Moon Bay, and the beach at Santa Cruz with its waterfront primed for sunsets. It meanders into the redwood forests and the rural outposts, where before too long the past catches up and stays in the shape of old wooden "teardowns" that haven't yet been. I ambled through numerous farmers' markets, where the perfume of homemade soaps and candles vied with the aromas from oven-fresh cakes and cookies. I took a trail through the Uvas Creek Country Park, an old lumber site where a picnic table was an artifact of historical graffiti.

I went wine-tasting in the hills somewhere less predictable than Napa or Sonoma, stayed in a cabin at America's oldest hostel, the Hidden Villa, a 1,600-acre working farm in the canyon of the Santa Cruz mountains, and walked up to hilltops where observatories chart the circuits of stars. On a cold, rainy January evening, I sat in an outdoors hot tub at the Pigeon Point Lighthouse. The ocean was lashing on the rocks, the beacon beating out the dark. Less than an hour away, Silicon Valley's traffic was keeping its own rush-hour rhythm.

The travel writer Martin Cheek was quick to spot the tourist potential of Silicon Valley. He produced the first authoritative handbook to the area, an array of people, places, and innovations, which addresses the dichotomy of the place, and its rapid acceleration. "There's a dynamic vitality to this region that makes it such an exciting and interesting place to explore. But this vitality is the dread of travel book writers," he notes.

But, the other attractions aside, the worldview of Silicon Valley is constructed from its technological bedrock, even if its communities are considerably older.

Over at KICU 36 in San Jose, Doug McKnight's "Silicon Valley Business" program has charted the fortunes of tech since 1993. The Moore's Law–driven economy is great TV. Start-ups, up-starts, the characters of companies and CEOs who, as Doug notes, are all very different. The program started broadcasting as Silicon Valley became a concept of revitalization during the postdepression. Now the talk is why some dot.coms fail while others succeed. Here, reporters pronounce "url" as a word, not u-r-l. Captions under interviewees carry web addresses.

KICU36 is owned by Cox Broadcasting, parent of the award-winning KTVU TV at Oakland just south of San Francisco. Its competition is KNTV's News Channel 11 also out of San Jose, with its own tech report, and the public broadcaster KTEH, part of PBS. Over in San Francisco, CNET Networks is a major technology information provider that has its own radio and TV programming.

Silicon Valley's captive commuter audiences can tune into San Jose's KBay (soft rock), KFOX (classic rock), KRTY (country),

KSJO (rock), and KSJS, which broadcasts out of San Jose State University.

Aside from the ever-expanding *San Jose Mercury News,* the word on the street in Silicon Valley comes from the free weekly *Metro,* or a half-dozen community newspapers—the *Campbell Reporter,* the *Cupertino Courier,* the *Los Gatos Weekly-Times,* the *Saratoga News,* the *Sunnyvale Sun,* and the *Willow Glen Resident*—as well as the *Thoi Bao Daily News,* the *Vietnam Daily News, El Observator,* and *La Oferta Review.*

THE PEOPLE

THE DEMOLITION DERBY |

For capitalists and farmers of the revenue, somewhat comfortable and showy apartments must be constructed, secure against robbery; for advocates and public speakers, handsomer and more roomy, to accommodate meetings; for men of rank who, from holding offices and magistracies, have social obligations to their fellow-citizens, lofty entrance courts in regal style, and most spacious atriums and peristyles, with plantations and walks of some extent in them, appropriate to their dignity. They also need libraries, picture galleries, and basilicas, finished in a style similar to that of great public buildings, since public councils as well as private law suits and hearings before arbitrators are very often held in the houses of such men.
—Vitruvius, *The Ten Books of Architecture,* book VI, chapter V

Marcus Vitruvius Pollio had a point. The Roman architect and engineer, writing in the first century B.C.E., could well transfer his shrewd observations to twenty-first-century Silicon Valley. The house defines the man, or woman, and few issues stir the blood more in this area than housing and the many variations on the theme that allows an address in a place frequently more costly than Manhattan. Often wired, occasionally weird, the Silicon Valley home can be a room, a shared house, an apartment, a cozy colonial, a roof-heavy family suburban, a Tudor-style one-storey, "a delightful CTGE (no pets)," a large pool with house attached, short-term apartment suites, a Victorian charmer, a fabulous view, a two-acre yard, a plot, a plan. In social terms, it's also a drop-in, a workplace, a den, a haven, a dot.com victory laurel, or a halter of unrealized financial expectation. Critiques are expected; it's open season on every domus from Hearstian architectural follies in their redefined landscapes to mansions hidden in the redwoods high above the Valley, buildings planted there in the first wave of innovation. In the midst of the soaring cost of real estate and rentals, seven-figure "tear-downs" have supplanted the wheeled-in salvage of historic buildings as out-of-towner curiosities. The trailers here are called mobile homes, and such is the demand for affordable housing they also have open house days, like regular sought-after houses. On the edge of this, the poorer communities of San Jose create home lives as best they can, steeling themselves against fires that arrive in the night and move them on to emergency shelters and other camps of uncertainty. Some of the homeless in Silicon Valley resist help, wheeling their cardboard walls and plastic bags containing their identities around the pristine streets of historic downtown, gathering in St. James Park, or finding salvation near the door of the cathedral.

In archaeology, deductions are made about habitations and their likely inhabitants from the material remains. The smudge of black is evidence of a hearth; demarcations of doors, openings, entrances, and exits help to build a picture of how the house was lived in and reconstruct paths through the rooms. Other evidence—pottery shards, bones, artifacts such as playthings, cookery items, residues of eating, socializing, bathing, praying—help to construct the social life of the house. The number of rooms and their size give clues to the number of inhabitants; objects give possibilities of their apparent gender, ages, and occupations. The presence of workshops, their debris and items of production define activity, large containers mark out storage areas, such as those at palatial residences at Knossos and Pylos in the Bronze Age Mediterranean. On the island of Delos, I was once shown evidence that pointed to a tavern with a brothel above which served the many merchants and seamen using the port. The top floor had crashed to the first over two thousand years, but the suggestion of sound and space remained. The artifacts that evidenced the brothel included coins from various foreign countries, and the remnants of women's rouge.

Anthropologists have an easier time of it deciphering domestic space. In her classic study of Mongolian nomads, Caroline Humphrey, an anthropologist at Cambridge University, England, charted striking changes over time and historical events, in the interior lay-out of a traditional tent, or yurt, on the Asian Steppes. She provided evidence of the material culture of the domestic space—furniture, objects, entrances—before and after the intro- duction of communism in the region. Most obvious in the later model was the absence of a shrine, the space now being occupied by a television set. In Silicon Valley, analysis of the layouts of re- designed older homes would include noting the number of outlets for computer terminals and DSL lines, evidence of cabling installa- tions, and receivers for wireless connections. And then there are the areas of transition that depend on an understanding of certain rules of etiquette and the selection of space by certain people. This would include areas of larger estates that are open to staff, demar- cated tradesmen's entrances, gardeners' cottages, guesthouses, and areas for valet parking. In his analysis, *The Victorian Country House,* the social anthropologist Mark Girouard highlighted those ways of using domestic space that have disappeared from contemporary use of the house, but remained etched in the memory of the place; the separate staircases for men and women, the gentlemen's smoking room, the ladies' withdrawing room; the maid's quarters; the children's nursery near the nanny's attic quarters. Leaving no physical traces, but reconstructed from performative memories, were such class-related rituals as servants playing "deaf" to conversation of the upper classes who employed them, reinforced by the practice of turning to the wall in certain parts of the house where they were held to be "invisible." Ishiguru's novel, *The Remains of the Day,* superbly defines the strata of domestics in an English country house between the World Wars.

Given the diversity of Silicon Valley culture, using a traditional methodology to analyze domestic architecture would not be too successful, but contemporary anthropologists could at least draw on testimony and observation—most particularly making comparative studies of changes over the past thirty years. Applying archaeological method is somewhat trickier. Without the benefit of knowing about booms and busts and how fortunes have been made in Silicon Valley, and left only with evidence of life there, obvious problems arise concerning the numbers of people living in houses, and also their social standing. Someone living all their life in an early house on a large lot in Palo Alto, for example, could easily find themselves next to a multimillionaire dot-commer who had paid cash for their first house. Probing the ruins, an archaeologist might find evidence in the wiring, should that survive. *The San Francisco Chronicle* of October 16, 2000 illustrates this perfectly in a story about celebrity neighborhoods. The report notes the person who moved into Steve Wozniak's childhood home—a four-bedroom Eichler house in Sunnyvale—said he could tell right away where the Apple pioneer had slept, as one of the bedrooms was extensively wired to support computers. The evidence is lost today. The house burned down and a new home was built on the site.

If we look at the foundations of buildings in Silicon Valley and apply the logic of domestic space defined by need, evidence would invariably be unreliable. Most notably, a large number of the more impressive and expensive, multiroomed homes are lived in by one, or sometimes two individuals. The extra rooms are designed for effect, giving a perception of more personal space than strictly necessary, and not part of everyday use. It's an extension of the form following function idea—these large homes are there to impress visitors, as Vitruvius suggests. Garages built to accommodate several cars may give a clue to the number of cars actually owned, or suggest the size of social life by providing guests with valet parking. Decadence is not always the reason, of course. There would also be occasions where the smaller home of choice—say, an apartment for a couple in a particular area—is not available, and the only property suitable in terms of cost or location is larger than actually required. In Silicon Valley, particularly, apartments are at a premium, the market affected by the high numbers of single tech-worker occupants working long hours, and who need little more than a base with benefit of onsite restaurants and recreation facilities.

If we consider the Pompeii effect again, the interiors of homes might well baffle archaeologists looking for a cultural assemblage. Within the rooms, the analysis of evidence provides a confusing picture, with decorator tastes taking further the design preferences of the owner or occupier, in a range of textures, colors, and artifacts reflecting the size of a budget more than the owners' personal tastes. The extended marketplace—including goods available over the internet—can create a bewildering array of cross-temporal and cross-cultural objects. In homes where decorators have not been at work, the contents may provide a more reliable clue to the preferences of the owners or tenants. A number of high-tech engineers have a passion for Pez dispensers (there is even a museum to that effect) and buy toys along with their hardware at Fry's.

Tom Jackiewicz's home is a good example of a tech worker's environment. His rented San Jose apartment is in a new block just off the historic old mission trail, the Alameda. He's about a grande cup away from a Starbuck's, and across the road there's a theater so old and unchanged, it's now tastefully retro. Tom, who moved across from Phoenix, Arizona in 1998, shares with another programmer, also called Tom, and his girlfriend who came over from Florida. It is a two-storey apartment. The sitting room features an impressive collection of toys, white walls, black and animal-print textiles. There is a set of black smoked-glass storage units once used to house parts of a now defunct NeXT computer, salvaged and finding new life as a storage stack for Tom and Tom's other computer hardware.

I catalog the items on their mantelpiece: one can of Budweiser, one tin of Spam (a mixed irony here of Monty Python humor—"The Spam Song"—and high-tech messaging—"spam" as in electronic junk mail); one gold alien model figure, one organic beer bottle, one bar of Star Wars Galactic glycerin soap, five playing cards; "Got Milk?" promotional model cow; a model shark; a model Pink Panther (playing bongos), a model penguin (Linux symbolism), one Austin Powers doll (boxed), one Dr. Evil doll (boxed); one model guy on skateboard promoting a clothes company; Felix the cat cartoon video; two Hardee's foods promotional toys, one a mouse strapped to a rocket; another cartoon mouse and cheese; three rubber models of a plumber, mechanic and toolman; one Looney Tunes floppy disc; two plastic spiders, two Blues Brothers badges, one model cow on bike, one model of heart-eyed girl; a rubber mobile phone, two packs of Pez candy, one lemon, one orange; five Pez dispensers—two Mickey Mouse, one Goofy, one Donald Duck, one witch; two more spiders; one cow and chicken game; one Felix the cat with fish; one unidentified wooden thing promoting "penguin power"; firelighters; one small furry animal; one Moving, Morphing, Modeling System plastic dinosaur; and one Marvin the Martian candy dispenser (rocket shaped).

Apart from the firelighters, which at least relate to the fireplace beneath the mantelpiece, the other items need some explanation if we play the Pompeii game. For example, while the amount of computer hardware in the apartment signals an occupation, or a preoccupation, some inside knowledge was needed for most of the mantelpiece material. Walking in cold, a computer programmer or engineer would most likely know the source of most of the mantel-piece material—Fry's store being a leading provider of geek play-things—and also recognize the promotional items picked up at trade shows or workplaces. But while the objects were vital signs, this apartment at least did not equate to a standard contemporary stereotype of high-tech workers being antisocial and unkempt in home and habits. In fact, Tom had begun house-hunting in earnest, in an up-market and historic area called the Rose Garden, a few blocks from his apartment.

Douglas Coupland has a fine time with geek household legend in *Microserfs,* in which he describes a property dubbed the "House of Wayward Mobility." Coupland writes: "Abe—our in-house millionaire, used to have tinfoil on all his bedroom windows to keep out what few rays of sun penetrated the trees until we ragged on him so hard he went out and bought a sheaf of black construc-tion paper at the Pay 'n' Save and taped it up instead. It looked like a drifter lived here."

On June 2, 2000, the *San Jose Mercury News* ran a story about the plight of janitors in Silicon Valley, some of whom were spend-ing nearly half their pay on rent. Reporter K. Oanh Ha noted: "The sought-after perks for these workers are health insurance, sick days and an annual salary that's more than a single digit." In Sep-tember, I walked around some of San Jose's poorest areas with Anthony Marek, Communications Director of the American Red Cross Santa Clara Valley Chapter. San Jose had been experiencing a series of fires; a couple of them were arson, others started by children playing with matches, or unwatched chip pans, or residents smoking in bed. Next to the burned-out carcass of a building that once represented several homes, a similar apartment block was renting for more than $1000 a unit. As many as ten people would be housed there. The ground was sticky with hot water gushing from a tap; the back yard was littered with refuse, the exterior unkempt and neglected. But a cursory glance through windows in this mainly Hispanic community revealed "home" was still there, in the gloom; a sense of place personified in religious pictures and votive objects, a television central and flashing. Children looked out from top windows, waved and darted away.

In the property pages of the *San Jose Mercury News,* I see an advert for an internet company—shedshop.com—that offers "The extra room you have always wanted . . . 83 practical uses for a residential shed." I wonder how literal the word "residential" could be.

There is also an advertisement for $6 million homes, and I am curious to see what this figure buys. The realtor, Ian McCrae, has been selling property for twenty-two years; he works as a broker for developers and, in keeping with most realtors in the United States, offers his properties on the internet, where potential clients can take a virtual tour. When Ian started out in business, Los Gatos was the proverbial sleepy little town. In 2000, with an average land cost of $2000 a square foot, high-end, multimillion-dollar homes are standard on the realtors' books. Also standard are features such as marble and granite kitchen and bathroom countertops, category 5 wiring to accommodate the latest high-tech specifications, a virtual environment of surround-sound cinema viewing, and in terms of aesthetics, "hardscaping," which creates an atmosphere of outdoors indoors.

Ian drives a white Cadillac, and a four-wheeler, both with personalized plates. He chooses the Cadillac to take me up in the hills above Los Gatos to a home described by its designer and owner as "Greek Plantation" style. The house has classical columns and banana plants off the drive at the front, and a Roman-style pool with torch lanterns and a pizza oven out the back. It has an eight-car garage, a waterfall fountain, and a guest house. The downstairs of the home is laid out, its Egyptian owner-designer tells me, so that he can see his children playing and watching TV from the vantage point of his study. The study itself is replete with replicas of Egyptian archaeological artifacts. A few rows of hieroglyphs, representing the family name, are painted on the study's white wall beneath a window. This comfortable room is the office and the family's technology nerve-center, with a large computer terminal, one of several pieces of high-tech hardware in the thoroughly wired house. The downstairs living space is open-plan; the three children can run through the house unimpeded by doors. The receptions areas are furnished in florals, and the spacious lobby has a large chandelier. The master bedroom has a sunken bath in its ensuite, and a fireplace. The property, which comes with two and a half acres of creek, across the road, is put on the market for $6 million.

A few minutes away I visit the home of Peter Tarrant, a forty-year-old British man, who lives alone in a house that offers a few clues to his English heritage. The first floor's plush Oriental furnishings, Japanese woodcuts, and raku pots, sumptuous textiles in milk-pale colors, and Peter's kitchen would also offer an archaeological conundrum in the shape of a Union Jack tea-mug. If we extract the story from this scene and view the evidence, it might appear that the inhabitant of this house is Asian and, given the large number of rooms, had a large family, or regular guests, one of whom could have presented him with this most distinctive symbol of British culture. In conversation with him, I learn that Peter is one of the real success stories of Silicon Valley's newcomers. Armed with a degree in electrical engineering, he first traveled to California in his job as a product manager for a British communications company. He stayed, was made vice president at thirty-four, became a millionaire at thirty-five and a multimillionaire five years later.

A few miles away, I find chatty senior Frank Lazouras by chance, after taking a wrong turn near Palo Alto. A road leads me along the Bayshore at Redwood City, and unexpectedly past a series of mobile home parks. Although I only intend to pull in to turn round, there is nowhere to move to, and so I drive through slowly, snaking through the well-maintained landscape of potted plants, plastic gnomes, and garden furniture clustered round the doors. These feel like homes in a traditional sense. I recall my early conversation with Josh from the trailer park at the bus stop in Santa Clara and wonder if anyone would agree to be interviewed. As I drive past one mobile, I notice its "For Sale" sign at about the same time as Frank gives me a friendly wave—passing drivers are infrequent round here. I park the car and greet him. It turns out he has just put his home on the market. He is moving to Florida after the death of his wife, and the sale in California will put money in his pocket and help him start over. The mobile is on the market for $75,000, and I tell him it sounds like a bargain. He tells me that he has bought a larger mobile in Florida for $12,500, with two bedrooms, two bathrooms, a sun room and air-conditioning. And it comes completely furnished. He has lived at his present home in Harbor Village for twenty-four years. He came to California from Rhode Island, a continent away, working as a journeyman and technician at the major electronics company, Ampex, from age eighteen until he retired in 1979. He and Florence moved to the mobile home park for some peace and quiet. When she developed cancer, he cared for her at home until the day she died. There is a quiet shrine to her in one corner, and her mauve dressing gown is still hanging off the wall in the bedroom. He says it's time for him to move, and at seventy-eight years old, he insists he will make the journey by car with a few things in a trailer, driving solo across America.

"House Demolition Sale." The sign alone is arresting. I'd been looking for a "tear-down" and anticipated a large house on a spectacular lot, not a regular family home, less than a century old, on a residential street in Los Gatos. When I arrived, the house was already partly dismembered; a couple was deliberating over a stone fireplace and eventually bought it and told me they would put it into storage until they had the right house. The company operating the sale has a whole yard full of house pieces—doors, floorboards, fittings. In Britain there's a long-established trade in period pieces from demolished homes—Victorian cast-iron fireplaces, ornamental radiators, Georgian paneling—but less predictable is the feverish ripping apart of presentable homes in a place where property is at a premium. It is understandable in economic terms; if someone is prepared to pay $1 million for a house only to demolish it, they are obviously ready to pay for a new house on a site. In terms of archaeology, the evidence of such behavior would be tricky to decipher. The discovery of a building in a partial tear-down state might suggest it is in a process of being refurbished; a total razing to the ground suggests a calamity. There would be no clues to a fire, or explosion. The neighboring properties still standing would rule out subsidence or earthquake. Only the tattered remains of a sign attached to a telegraph pole would provide the clue: "This way to Demolition Sale."

Back at the $6 million house two months later, considerable interest has not resulted in a sale. The price is dropped by $1 million and Ian McCrae organizes a realtors' "Open House." A procession of realtors arrive, in twos and threes, drop their business cards on the lobby table and go through the rooms.

North of Los Gatos, in Atherton, which competes for the title of more millionaires per square mile than any other part of Silicon Valley, a two-thirds scale French chateaux had just been sold. "Chez Amis" had a guide price of more than $5 million. It is set in landscaped gardens and has had just two owners since it was built in the 1920s. It has retained most of its period fittings, but the realtors tell me the new owners will employ a specialist architect to restore the original replica features.

A drive up one of the most glorious interstates in the United States, the 280, reveals nests of homes clustered around the redwoods. At Woodside, where the local stores have the look of a heritage site, residents are content to wind a path up the mountains, past the County Park and into a labyrinth of driveways to highly selective properties. The larger than life Jim Warren, founder of the West Coast Computer Fayre, and a hero of computer history, can survey the view down to the Pacific from his hot-tub. He was famously interviewed in it for the television program "The Triumph of the Nerds," and managed to persuade his interviewer to also take the plunge. However, I get to talk to Jim in more formal surroundings, sprawled on the seating in the round sitting room, a den that glows with the color of redwoods. He takes me on a tour. Predictably, there is a range of tech-ware in Jim's workshop; in other rooms there are houseguests, in fact his live-in programmer friends. The bathroom has an ocean-view to die for.

Back in the immensely conducive space of the sitting room, Jim is on a roll. We talk about creativity in computing, the culture of programming, the Homebrew Club and how things have changed from those days when people shared resources and innovation. "There was a feeling no other place in the nation had," he says, "and it was significantly spring-boarded off the cultural rebellion of the 1960s." I consider Jim's place—"a wired house in the woods"—which he had custom made twenty years ago, still has that feel of old wave high-tech. "We wanted to stand on each other's shoulders, not each other's toes." Jim's eyrie, which he leaves only when he has to, is a place where a transistor radio would still feel at home.

In a quiet street in San Jose, brothers Johnny and Mike Malone lean over the balcony of the apartment they have shared for fifty years. Every morning they have looked out on the same wooden houses, framed by the same trees, as around them the world—and their locality—has been turning somersaults. These are true survivors of the old and new technology age. Born on the East Coast, Johnny, aged eighty-two, and his seventy-two-year-old brother, were brought up in an orphanage in New York City. Johnny was in the Air Force and came to San Jose more by accident than design. He loves to tells the story of how after his discharge, he leapt aboard a Greyhound with his duffel bag and told the driver "I'll get off where the bus stops!" He worked on a chicken range in Campbell, when it was a farm landscape, in exchange for free rent, and lived for three years in Santa Cruz, working as a busboy. He came back to Santa Clara Valley to work at a fiberglass factory, and brought his brother over. They moved into the apartment block when it was new and now work there as caretakers of the property. They have known three landlords, and by working at one time for an asphalt plant, can be said to have literally helped build Silicon Valley. Inside their pin-neat apartment, pictures of the Pope and religious objects testify to their Irish Catholic background. The brothers still attend church, either locally at St. Leo's or the grander basilica of St. Joseph's in downtown San Jose. As close as brothers can be, it is hard to imagine a cross word between them. They say their lives have been blessed by the Catholic charities, and guardian angels.

Margaret O'Reilly is a realtor in the office of Alain Pinel in downtown Palo Alto. I first spoke with her in January 2000, when the market had shown forty percent price rises in four months. The people buying were often paying cash for the properties from stock options. Sometimes the younger ones, in their twenties and thirties, were moving directly from single rooms in shared housing to multimillion-dollar, fully wired homes, with swimming pools and customized fittings. The market was pushed up by proximity to good schools, but also by the reality of more buyers than houses.

When I contacted with her again in mid-October, the market was showing a response to the stock market falls. If not a flip to a buyers' market, there were signs that the upward trajectory of prices was being affected by the dot.com failures and values wiped off high-tech stock, although on a daily basis offers seem to be a little dependent on the stock market. "Yesterday there was a house in prime area of Palo Alto that had three offers, not one of which was over the asking price! This is most unusual, but the stock market has been heading down this week."

But her email included one of those stories that seems could only happen in Silicon Valley: "Last weekend there was a new listing I wanted to show in Woodside, but I couldn't make an appointment to show my clients until after Yom Kippur. I found out on Tuesday morning that it sold the night before. Supposedly some interested clients jogged on the road until they met the owners and proceeded to offer all cash and almost a million over if they signed a contract that night!"

October 26, 2000. The front page of the *San Jose Mercury News* is dominated by a story that has everyone talking. It's about a property with the title of Santa Clara County's biggest home. The terracotta-roofed Mediterranean-style home has five bedrooms, ten bathrooms, and a thirty-five car garage. The 18,000 square feet of living space extends over a six-acre lot looking down to San Francisco Bay. Named "Rancho San Antonio" when it was built sixty-one years ago by a General Motors tycoon, it then cost a sizable

$111,798. It features stone brought in from down the coast at
Carmel, marble hewn from quarries in Italy, and golden timbers
from first-cut redwood, indigenous to the area. SJMN reporter
Tracey Kaplan notes that "Silicon Valley magnates are erecting
what appear to be equally grand estates, at the same time as an
acute shortage of housing afflicts the region's middle-class and
low-wage workers, and prices spiral out of sight." Cindy and Gay-
mond Schultze bought the sprawling mansion in the Los Altos
Hills for $6 million in 1997. Three years later it's worth an esti-
mated $15 million. Gaymond Shultze—"who grew up milking
cows on a farm"—made his fortune when he sold Stratacom, the
telecommunications company he founded, to Cisco Systems for
$4.5 billion. He now has a networking equipment company, Vina
Technologies.

The place could even be described as a second home. For five
months of 2000, the Schultzes were far away from their Silicon
Valley idyll, sailing in the Mediterranean. The couple expect to
resume the trip when their new yacht is completed. Three years
ago, Cindy Schultze was a secretary at Hewlett-Packard, sharing a
two-bedroom cottage in West Valley with a roommate. Now her
home includes a master suite with two Greek columns, and a "hers"
bathroom that features toilet paper stamped with a gold mono-
grammed "S." Furniture has to be custom-made to suit the larger
dimensions. A plan to install a home theater has slowed up because
of a shortage of contractors. Cindy told Kaplan: "There's so much
money in Silicon Valley it takes forever to get anything done."

The "biggest home" title comes from Santa Clara County's
property tax records of 318,009 single-family detached homes, and
62,254 condominiums. But speed is everything. Kaplan adds that
less than a mile from the Schultzes an apparently larger mansion—
with fifteen bathrooms, for a family of five—is just weeks away
from completion.

The Schultze fortune was made in the heady days of the early internet boomtime. On the same front page that has a full-color picture of the tangible proceeds of that Gold Rush, a headline spells out another reality of fall 2000. "The thrill is gone at Internet show," it reads, providing a further note on "the ongoing dot.com shake out." The Internet World forum in New York had more exhibitors than 1999, but Chris O'Brien reports: "Gone is the revolutionary rhetoric of past years. It's been replaced by talk about how to survive while making improvements that seem downright incremental compared with much of the hype once associated with the Internet."

The recycling of land—or land reuse—is another factor that needs consideration in an archaeological survey of Silicon Valley. In the Old World, the reuse of city sites resulted in tells, ancient mounds as large as hills that would take a lifetime to excavate. They were formed by the building and razing of urban centers over millennia, and as such provide immensely valuable evidence of change. The burning of cities, such as Troy, left stratified scars on the landscape. The repositioning of urban or cultural places identifies their relative importance, showing how environmental changes led to abandonment of certain areas, sometimes followed by later redevelopment and a return to earlier glory. At Tell-el Amarna, in Egypt, the idiosyncratic pharaoh Amenhotep IV, otherwise known as Ahkenaten, built a new city on a desert site to glorify his monotheistic rule. The sun was central to his religion, and buildings had courtyards to capture as much of the sun's rays as was possible. His designs called for major irrigation works to support his desire for luxuriant gardens and agriculture, but the ecology of the region worked against him, and after his death the city was abandoned.

CROSSING CULTURES |

My programmers are using an English language compiler to write
their programs, but looking over their work I still don't know what
they are doing. Because English is cumbersome and highly redundant,
they end up with a set of abbreviations which I cannot understand. . . .
The slightest variation from the proscribed English language form
causes the computer indigestion.
—John H. Hughes, Assistant Vice President, Systems and Programming, American Mutual Liability Insurance Company, speaking at
MIT centenary lecture series, 1961

[W]e run into that too, particularly the tendency of programmers to
abbreviate, misspell, and forget periods at the ends of sentences. The
first thing we did was to invent a young lady called a "pseudocoder"
and put her in charge of all abbreviations. No one was allowed to use
an abbreviation unless it was registered with her. . . .
—Grace Hopper, programming pioneer and former senior mathematician, Eckert-Mauchly Computer Corporation, responding

From a discussion titled "A New Concept in Programming," part of the
MIT centenary lecture series, 1961, published first as *Management and
the Computer of the Future,* then as *Computers and the World of the Future.*

The problem posed by the diversity of programming languages was central to the discussion at MIT in those early days of computing. In 1961, the enduring symbol of unintelligibility, the Tower of Babel, was chosen for the cover by the august journal, the *Communications of the Association for Computer Machinery.* Each brick in the tower signified a different programming language. Programs were being produced at the rate of 300 million words a year, a statistic that left one discussant "interested and somewhat stunned." There was what was described as "a programming bottleneck." Academic and engineer George Brown, Director of the Western Data Processing Center at UCLA, told the panel: "Every university machine that I have ever seen gets filled up right away." The distinctive symbol of tongues not speaking a common language was entirely appropriate.

Today in Silicon Valley, it is the words on the streets, rather than in the labs, that do not always connect. Older Hispanic and Vietnamese who have missed out on learning English rely on their grandchildren to translate. Signs in public places, such as on Valley transit buses, are written in American English, Vietnamese, and Spanish. Most ATMs and recorded telephone messages have Spanish options. The *San Jose Mercury News* publishes editions in Spanish and Vietnamese.

Tech workspaces reflect the diversity of populations, as do the areas of Silicon Valley that are social and cultural hubs for workers from other countries. Castro Street in Mountain View is a stretch of diverse Asian eating houses. In San Jose, Japantown is an area architecturally replete with temples, restaurants, and food stores. California has always had a strong Pacific Rim and Spanish population. Now the tech boom has brought in huge numbers of engineers from Southern Asia, notably India. It is a phenomenon with roots in an ancient cultural practice. As *Christian Science Monitor* reporter Robert Marquand reports:

South Asians pride themselves on what in modern parlance is called "left brain" or logical and disciplined thinking. As a whole they excel in math, memory skills, and reciting complex patterns.

Many Indian parents wake up their kids as early as 4 A.M. to start recitation, memorization, or homework. . . . Some analysts say that an emphasis on memory and math is part of the Brahminical legacy in India. Brahminical learning stresses memorization of thousands of pages of Sanskrit texts and shlokas, two line couplets from the Hindu Vedas. ("In India, obsession with trivia is a lifeline," reprinted in *San Jose Mercury News,* November 8, 2000)

May, 2000. I am intrigued by the sound of "Sikhism in Cyberspace," a paper to be given in a conference at the College of Engineering, San Jose State University. There is a scattering of non-Sikhs but the culture is well represented by vast numbers of the turbans and saris, and by the aroma of lunchtime curry distributed freely to all. I speak with a Sikh high-tech engineer who is a third-generation member of his family's move to the old Santa Clara Valley. "My Grand-uncle came to the area in 1905, as a farm laborer. There was a scarcity of land in the Punjab and the area was still under the influence of British 'rule.' The United States represented freedom." Changes over time had shifted the work base, the skills required, and the positioning of Sikhs in local society.

"Twenty years ago, life was very tough. Racism and discrimination. Sikhs cut hair to keep jobs. Not a very positive image because of poverty in India. But education was very important." I suggest he can keep in contact with old friends and relatives by email. But there is no internet in his village back home. Most of his family now lives in Silicon Valley.

There are around 7,000 Sikhs in San Jose, between 40,000 and 50,000 in the San Francisco Bay Area; 100,000 in the state of California. A new temple in Fremont would complement the thirty-five elsewhere in the state. "We are able to carry on culture and religion—whenever we see people together it gives us so much strength from each other."

October 2000. Coffee-break at the prestigious SiliconIndia.com conference in San Jose. It's held at the city's high-end venue of the Fairmont Hotel. The air is sparky with electronic conversation, and conversations on electronics. Faced with a phalanx of predominantly male Indian entrepreneurs talking into cell phones, I ask to be pointed in the direction of a high-powered woman. All eyes lead to an imposing figure in a red embroidered suit. Vani Kola. Originally from Hyderabad in southern India, she received her engineering degree from Arizona. She's a mover and shaker in the thrusting field of business-to-business exchange.

In fact she's so sought after, the only time I can catch her is on the way to the women's restroom. Yes, Vani Kola performs a formidable juggling act. She raises a family, but it's soon clear that such points are pretty immaterial as a point of discussion here. "I never see myself as a 'woman'—I'm a person, there are no barriers!" We pause at the restroom door, and continue the conversation inside. Even in these cozy, perfumed environs, Vani holds the stage. "This is an entrepreurism, capitalism, innovation-oriented society. Gender is a secondary factor." A younger Indian woman looks on, enthralled. It becomes clear why Vani is such a power-broker. "After all, if a woman is successful and breaks down the professional barrier, she becomes one of the guys." She chats with the young woman and then Vani has to go.

India's soaraway success in terms of technology has effected another social change—the demand for the highly sought after work visas called the H1-B. In November 2000, the *San Jose Mercury News,* in conjunction with SiliconIndia, investigated and published a special report on the visa issue. While the quota for H1-Bs had been raised in the fall, the promise of salaries unheard of in India had created a serious problem of fraud and exploitation. There existed a middleman market for visas, and with that attendant opportunities for an abuse of the system. There was a significant argument for overhauling it.

The young woman so keen to chat with Vani Kola catches up with me as I head across the Fairmont lobby. She wants to find out more about my research. Over the next half hour it is her story that rivets me to a chair. Thirty-two-year-old Nita Sanil had been in Silicon Valley for three years. But Nita's was not the traditional trajectory from Indian city or village to the palm trees of San Jose.

Back in Bombay, she had taken a degree in child development, and began work doing market research for Samir, affiliated with one of India's largest advertising agencies. "Advertising was just evolving in India," she said. "I asked a lot of questions about it and went back to college to study it." At twenty, she was an advertising executive at a small start-up advertising agency, Percept, and was promoted twice in one year. She left for another even more high-profile agency and her success seemed guaranteed. She had married young and her husband was keen to come to the United States. After two visa rejections, she arrived in Dayton, Ohio. Nita took a Masters in communication and published a research paper on organ donation and persuasion strategy. "My brother had kidney failure in India. It inspired me to study strategies that persuaded people to donate an organ. My hypothesis was supported. I am proud of that achievement."

Nita's husband became an entrepreneur and the couple moved to Silicon Valley, where she sold software solutions for Franz, Inc. The seven-year marriage did not survive. "I felt I had failed my culture," she said. She resolved to stay in the Valley but says she was dogged by immigration problems and uncertainty. Her determination to be part of the tech boom involved working for start-ups, but she says she was countered by exploitation and employers abusing the insecurity of the H1-B visa situation. "I was taken advantage of. I would overachieve my sales quota but still not receive recognition or title." After a trip back to India, during which her father died, Nita came back to no job. "For the first time, I thought I was set up in my career, and they fired me. It left me feeling helpless but determined to position myself for success."

Undaunted, she started work for another small start-up. She became a volunteer Public Relations Officer for TIEcon, an organization for budding entrepreneurs. Her cellphone goes off a few times, people come by wanting to speak with her. She says goodbye to me with a shake of a beautifully hennad hand. "Just the one painted?" I ask, "What's the significance?" "My friend's wedding—I didn't have time to get the other done!"

In Saratoga, the Hakone Japanese Gardens pose another cultural conundrum. This public space was founded in 1918 by Oliver and Isabel Stine, two art patrons from San Francisco, who were inspired by botanical displays at the Panama Pacific Exhibition. After Isabel traveled to the Fuji-Hakone National Park in Japan she created a model garden back in northern California. In time, archaeological excavators may be mystified by the reproduction of a nineteenth-century Kyoto tea-merchants' house and shop. It was prefabricated in Japan using traditional tools, and shipped to Saratoga. It now functions as a cultural exchange center. The gardens have always been popular with visiting Japanese, and often form a backdrop for wedding photographs. All the more nowadays with the growing number of Japanese high-tech employees and their families. A traditional tea ceremony is still performed. Japanese high-tech workers represent two percent of H1-B visa holders according to figures in November 2000.

British workers take up another two percent. And those workers who prefer their tea to be the Earl Grey variety, rather than green, head for an address in Campbell. Here the HP sauce is to do with London's Houses of Parliament rather than skittish workers at Hewlett-Packard.

Inside its hallowed walls, there are the brands of nostalgia that make the British heart beat faster—Cadbury's chocolate, which always comes up in the new settlers' ex-patriated conversation about longed-for foods, Heinz baked beans, Golden Shred marmalade. There are freezers filled with steak and kidney pies—Americans not being big on offal, apparently—pork pies, and shepherd's pies. Many are made locally to British recipe. "The stuff of memories," as Bill Fredlund would put it. An American retired fighter pilot with an English wife, he wisely realized a few years back there was more to be made importing British foods to the United States than British antique furniture.

It all started with Heinz salad cream. "People would ask me to get it when I went over. I made around five trips a year. I'd bring the salad cream in with the furniture. Then I decide to concentrate on food instead."

From fifteen items, the British Store now carries more than 3000 products. Customer loyalty is huge and a flourishing mail-order list ensures an interesting redistribution of British foods around California. The crates are loaded in Liverpool and each new supply is eagerly greeted. Last in were 800 Christmas puddings. "When I'm over I check out the supermarkets for new products. Sometimes people ask for specific things," says Bill.

As I am sighing with nostalgia for the items on the shelves, I realize my Proustian memories are going further back than a few months. Some products I swear I haven't seen in Britain since childhood. "That's true," says Bill. "Often people ask how I've tracked down something even they couldn't find in England."

The British Food Center is pretty much a community hub for the British community. There are signs to help the ex-pat techie hold on to his or her Scottish, Welsh, English, and Northern Irish roots. Bumper stickers proclaim cultural solidarity.

Cliché as it sounds, the shelves do hold supplies of Brown Betty teapots, kettles, tea-cosies, and teacups. There are lines of romantic novels, the type probably penned in some windswept cottage in the Yorkshire Dales. There are Enid Blyton children's books, charming Queen Mother souvenirs, and videos of the quintessential British TV soap, Coronation Street. In fact an archaeologist excavating the British Food Center would be able to glimpse not so much what is important in British culture, as what British people abroad think is important in British culture. There are items with no American parallel—twenty-first birthday keys, wedding horseshoes, and greetings cards for significant days others than Thanksgiving. Different takes on Christmas and Easter, good wishes from a sceptered isle where "happy holiday" is kept in the singular.

It is also a place of support. When Diana, Princess of Wales, died, the center became a kind of shrine, a place of pilgrimage that had its own signing book.

The clientele are not limited to Brits with cravings. "American people come to try the food, especially the sweets." Or should that be candy?

The place is full of fancy-that stories. Bill imports his Coca-Cola from the U.K. for a start. And in a wonderful Silicon Valley twist, one of the big sellers is a range of Indian foods, made for the expanding South Asian population in England, and appropriated into British culture. Now exported from Liverpool, across the world to California, to be sold just down the road from Fremont and Mountain View with their Indian products from across the Pacific.

BETTER TO FAIL HOPEFULLY . . . |

> We're getting ready to sell our six-person office setup (cubes, chairs, whiteboards, bookshelves, worktables cabinets, etc.) and startup hardware (developer PCs, docking stations, monitor, firewall PC, extension cords, networking cables, spare keyboards/mice, etc.). Besides going through Ebay, does anyone have suggestions of how/where to sell our things? We are in San Mateo, California, and would prefer if possible to sell locally. Thanks for any help.
> —Message posted at Startupfailures.com discussion site, November 2000

The recycling of computers puts one set of materials back into the system as reusable goods. A new social phenomenon recycles not just computers but people, their skills, and their ability to pick themselves up, dust themselves down—and start all over again.

The year 1999 saw the beginning of a new phase in Silicon Valley culture, the dot.bomb. With it came a brave new site—Startupfailures.com—that addresses the need for a forum and space for those who have plunged to earth like Icarus in the internet e-business dive. The site's slogan says it all—"the place for bouncing back." It features stories of entrepreneurs who have hit the heights and fallen, but got to their feet again. Contained within is information on services and resources to help practically in terms of dealing with debts and furniture sales, and psychologically, to deal with the trauma of failing in a place where everyone else seems to be succeeding.

"That's one of the critical needs of the entrepreneur. Emotional support." I'm talking to Startupfailure founder Nicholas Hall at his home high above the Castro Valley. It's a glorious location, and it seems distanced just enough from the Machiavellian complexities of the power-rooms of the inner Silicon Valley. From this eyrie, the personable Hall seems to breathe and exhale a different air. "There is a tremendous amount of failure in the Valley," he says with refreshing honesty. "It can be tougher than losing a marriage. One questions confidence, belief in oneself." Hall should know. He has been involved in three start-up failures. He is, however, happily married.

Hall was inspired to found Startupfailures after reading an article that chronicled the ups and downs of his fellow entrepreneurs. The article mentioned the daunting statistics of startup failures. Hall recognized the need to acknowledge the toll borne by those who had tried, tried, and tried again.

Hall was a stranger to the sprawling Silicon Valley and its mores, but not its business practices. He and his wife moved to California from Ohio. There he had started his career at Price Waterhouse and in time founded three companies. In 1998, he was the youngest recipient of the Cincinnati Business Courier's Top 40 Under the Age of 40 award for outstanding leadership. Hall was an active leader with the Ohio Society of CPAs, and in 1997, he was one of the youngest participants in the national CPA vision project.

Hall grew up in a town of 15,000 people. He admits he has retained his midwestern values and perspective. "I come from a huge part of the world that isn't 'connected'—isn't as easy with the fax, cell phone or email etiquette." He welcomes the way technology connects people—not least through his own website—but he is wary of Silicon Valley hype, its overbelief in itself and its ethereal and intangible products. Balance and checking is vital. In this way the "failures" can be measured in terms of the visionaries and entrepreneurs whose apparent failure was part of their path to success. A reassuring passage from Thomas Edison greets visitors to the Startupfailures.com home page:

> Results? Why, man, I have gotten lots of results! If I find 10,000 ways something won't work, I haven't failed. I am not discouraged, because every wrong attempt discarded is another step forward. Just because something doesn't do what you planned it to do doesn't mean it's useless. . . . Reverses should prove an incentive to great accomplishment. . . . There are no rules here, we're just trying to accomplish something.

Its founder continues: "Startupfailures is the first community focused on supporting individuals that have recently gone through or are going through the experience of a startup failure. Our purpose is to take the stigma out of failing and to help you recover quickly from a failure and get back into the game and in action. The only true failure is never trying."

Learning how to fail is part of the rite of passage to success in Silicon Valley. But Hall admits it isn't easy, and too often people lose perspective of what is important. It's the half-empty, half-full glass conundrum—failure can liberate and allow reshaping and regrowth, or it can cause acute embarrassment, and can damage physically and emotionally. "People who have failed can be wound up in a world of hurt," says Hall. That the website exists is enough for some who feel acutely alone in their situation.

The website believes in the entrepreneurial spirit. Indeed, Hall is president of the Silicon Valley Association of Software Entrepreneurs, a movers and shakers group that hosts regular power breakfasts and networking events.

The Startupfailures discussion board bristles with messages on subjects ranging from specific dot.bombs, to the practical matter of disposing of the material culture of a closed-down operation. Hall may be no stranger to startup failure, but he says he has always enjoyed the journey in good times and the bad. Next to Hall's photo on the site, a biographical note says he has gained from the ride: "his health, well being and relationships have grown stronger as his entrepreneurial journey continues."

Startupfailures has a coaching service help the entrepreneur refocus on their skills and strengths, to create a vision and develop a plan to attain it—"stop doing what you dislike or are not good at!" All this while balancing work and personal life. This is an important issue in Silicon Valley, where the leeching of work into home life, notably through the constant connectivity of emails, cell phones, and beepers, is endemic. These tools of personal connection exist together with broader aspects of Silicon Valley material culture, those that broadcast the buzz of the moment to insiders and outsiders of the tech revolution, from hoardings to the most incremental of NASDAQ movements trickling on a TV screen.

Hall works from an office at home. Before starting Startupfailures he had already started out on the visionary path, as the inventor of the critically acclaimed *Future Scrapbook.* It's a series of texts and exercises, a visionary handbook—"May you have the design of your life," he writes. One of his heroes is the British entrepreneur and Virgin pioneer, Richard Branson.

True to form, Hall visualized moving to California with his wife, and quickly achieved it. "By creating a scrapbook of your future you transform your dreams and goals from flashes in your mind or word scratched on a piece of paper to real tangible evidence for their achievement. The *Future Scrapbook* makes your aspirations appear real. If the human mind believes that a dream is real, then it is achievable."

Hall reminds me of the little boy who pointed out the emperor had no clothes. In the midst of one of the most conspicuously consumptive and materialistic places in America, Hall is saying: "Having stuff doesn't make you happy." This is no idealist hermit living in a cabin in the wood—though one imagines Hall and his wife, Jennifer, would rise to the outback challenge. He's a man who believes it's OK to be successful and proud of it, but who accepts that not succeeding is also part of the game. Just move on.

Back to the question posed at the top of this section, seen on the Startupfailures discussion board. One answer posted in response was simple, illuminative, and a great example of Silicon Valley recycling: Sell your office equipment to . . . another start-up.

SOCIAL STRIFE |

A dry, medium hopped auburn beer with a mildly sweet finish. The beer originates from Bavaria where it was brewed in March ("marz" in German) and stored in caves to be drunk during hot weather. We hope you'll enjoy it year round.
—Label on Marzen, brewed in San Jose, California, by the Gordon Biersch Brewing Company

Entrée prices in Silicon Valley have broken the $50 barrier . . .
—A story in Silicon Valley Life section, *San Jose Mercury News,* May 17, 2000

Tom Jackiewicz is trying to find the entrance to his friend's apartment. The black dice are swinging in the new Jaguar he's driving as he sashays around the complex car park. He's on the cell phone. "Where? You can see me? That's cool! You can really see me?" He parks and, still talking into the phone, gets out and heads into the labyrinth. I'm in tow, entirely in Tom's hands for a Saturday night out, Silicon Valley style.

I've been working up to this on various occasions in San Jose. The Flying Pig Irish bar—all open fire and pints of the dark stuff—some great Spanish and Peruvian restaurants, and a

From left: Tom Williams, Adam Lyons, and Tom Jackiewicz,
downtown San Jose, January 2000.

nightclub where the dance floor was packed with techies who
I figured had more on their person than I had in my bank account.

At least the techies were on the dance floor. I hear tales of social
lives so lacking in the social part that netiquette involves after-
shave. Even the *San Jose Mercury News* has taken up the cause of the
highly paid but solitary tech worker in an advertisement for its
entertainment pages. The cliché of long hours and absorbing projects has become part of the perception of Silicon Valley. That way
of life exists for sure. A friend of Tom's joined us for coffee once,
arrived with his PowerBook and didn't stop coding all evening.
Uncertainty over dot.coms makes those still reaping the rewards
even more intense.

But that's not the whole story. The nights may not be long, but
Silicon Valley's bars and restaurants see plenty of business. Cell
phones and pagers direct the social traffic. Distance is no object.
Especially in a comfortable car.

Tom is in need of a good night out. He is waiting on a start-up
deal after a venture capitalist pulled out $15 million when the
stock market jittered. He's quit smoking, taken up the gym. He
looks cool.

His pal Steve opens the door in ecstatic mood. He is wearing a new silk shirt from Macy's. "Great deals!—saw three for $50!" Steve works in sales and marketing. They could have sold tickets for the virtuoso performance he gives in his living room. He stands and delivers his pitch. His line moves from tech business to women. And the problem of finding them. "The thing is if you find someone you like, you've got to get her to notice real quick or it may be three months before another one you like comes along . . ." Tom's nodding in agreement. In Silicon Valley, the bucks are big, but true romance remains a precarious startup. "I was going to spend $2000 on this girl's birthday and she called and said she couldn't make it. You know what? I just took those emerald earrings back to Macy's . . ."

Steve's still talking as we're heading out the door and into the car. We go to a waterfront restaurant south of San Francisco. At the bar we drink margaritas and eat oysters, and Steve and Tom window shop the female waiters. The place is packed with well-heeled diners. The menu is unpretentious—Caesar salad, clam chowder, fish. Tom explains that the variation on the theme that is "chicken Caesar" is quintessential Silicon Valley—"Easy and quick to eat, and pretty healthy with that extra edge of protein." As the waiter clears away, an overladen backhand delivers a trickle of oily salad dressing down the back of Steve's new silk shirt. The waiter apologizes and returns with soda water. He dabs Steve's back. Tom looks at the damage. Steve's not impressed. The check arrives. Steve tells the waiter he wants a new shirt. The waiter returns with an "Oops, we goofed!" slip and an offer to pay for dry cleaning, refunded in thirty days.

"Thirty days!" says Steve, rising to the performance, "I want to take this shirt to Orlando tomorrow!" Steve goes to find the manager. His skill at closing deals pay off. The check is picked up by the restaurant. We go to leave and Steve says: "OK, we'd better leave the waiter a tip." He looks at Tom. Tom leaves $20. "Hey, man why did you leave $20?" Steve looks incredulous. Tom says: "That's the only note I had!" The waiter is delighted, if rather confused, at this unexpected generosity.

We drive down the freeway to Burlingame. The drive-in cinema is showing "Toy Story 2." Woody stands twenty-feet-tall against the clear Bay nighttime sky. Burlingame used to be best known for its sheer number of car dealerships. Now smart people populate its plethora of brewhouses, high-end restaurants, and bars. Burlingame is a key player in the Silicon Valley singles game. We move from place to place, Steve and Tom maxing their search engines. For once, this mother lode of lively young singles proves disappointing. We leave Burlingame for a trawl further down the Peninsula.

We pull up at an Italian steak house and lounge. The chairs are red leather. The clientele is old valley. A quartet of blonde women in tee-shirts and shorts chat animatedly, elderly couples sway to generic tunes on the dance floor. We barely get the seats warm when Steve wants to move on. Next stop, the Ramada Inn. But the Hacienda-style bar is empty. We head for the Russian place down the road. It's closed. Back in the car, I realize that Tom and Steve are playing new money anarchists. They figure I could go to any Mexican-style, mission, minimalist, pan-Pacific, or just plain cool bar any evening, anywhere in the dot.com bandwidth. This is an alternative experience. We drive past a bikers' lounge. A few minutes later, we drive back again. "This could be cool." The windows are steamed up. There's a crowd dancing to a Latin band. The dress code is leather, kerchiefs, and tight jeans. The pool tables are booked out, so we have a few games of darts.

I don't hear a cell phone or pager all night. I tell the guys how refreshing it is to be in a regular bar in Silicon Valley, without the high-earner posse. "Are you kidding?" says Steve. "Those aren't normal bikers' bikes out front—must have cost $30,000 or $40,000 apiece!'

The business and pleasure cocktail is a favorite in Silicon Valley. For many, the point of going to the newest bar or club is to rub shoulders with other techie wunderkinds. For recruiters and professional networkers, it's their job.

I get talking to Chris Davenport at the Brewhouse in Los Gatos. She is pale blond, immaculately groomed, and fully armed with pager and cell phone. It turns out she is a tech recruiter with a specialization—top-flight British personnel. She is primed by companies looking for key people. Suffice it to say that money is not the issue here. A greater part of Chris's work is socializing and her key places are the bars where British people gather. By day she works from her office at home, garnering an exhaustive list of contacts. She proves a tough interview. Nice as pie, she is rarely off the phone or can be distracted from her terminal.

One of the Valley's prime networking spots is a bar and restaurant called "The Basin" in downtown Saratoga. It is connected with one of the founders of Netscape. On an outside wall is its passionate mission statement: "This establishment was conceived and created in the entrepreneurial spirit of Silicon Valley; a belief that given a positive workplace, and a commitment to excellence, people of diverse talents can gather together and build a better product. We incite you to experience a taste of why we love to live and work in Northern California. Welcome to the Basin, established 1999."

In ancient Greece, the high-rollers attending the classical symposia watered down their wine in vast containers called kraters. In that way they could moderate the flows of quality conversation and alcoholic consumption. Undiluted alcohol was the province of the so-called barbarians of northern Europe. According to the ancient writer Strabo, in the first century B.C.E., the northern Celtic tribes imported vast quantities of wine from the Mediterranean world in exchange for salt, slaves, and fine hunting dogs.

Silicon Valley culture seems to have more in common with the Greeks, possibly aided by the tough U.S. liquor laws. Rounds of private parties marked the heyday of the dot.coms in the late 1990s. In more uncertain times balance is everything. If networking provides the place to drink, there is certainly little time to recover. In the summer of 2000, "the cliché cocktail of choice for the dot.com party set," according to style watchers Tracy Seipel and Michelle Quinn, was vodka combined with Red Bull, a nonalcoholic "energy drink" containing vitamins and amino acids: ". . . a potent combination that gets him wired and drunk at the same time" (*San Jose Mercury News,* June 2, 2000, p. 3c).

It's an interesting implication of this news item that the cocktail imbiber will be male. The outsider's impression of Silicon Valley, borne out in articles in the international press, is that it is overrun with single men looking for a partner. And further, that the area has become a magnet for predatory females. In reality, a large number of those employed in tech are married with families. Of the remainder, a large percentage, further than not having time to find a partner, do not regard it as a priority. Those actively looking rely on friends and business connections, or turn to introduction agencies as they would recruiters in the work environment. Julie Paiva started Table for Six in San Francisco fifteen years ago as a way of putting busy people in touch. As demand grew, she opened a branch in the center of Silicon Valley. She has 4000 members in the greater Bay Area, 2000 of them in Mountain View. There's a one-to-one ratio of men to women.

"There are no more workaholics in the Bay Area than in the rest of the country," she says. "They are trying to make their first million, and it's hard!" Not least when they are distracted by the ups and downs of the tech industry over this past year. "And often they are people far from family and friends. They come to me because they want to date outside the industry. Otherwise they may only meet new people at work-related activities. They are tired of working 24/7 and talking about it socially."

Julie's team also focuses on the individual's broader picture, as image consultants and relationship advisors. She counters the way techies are often represented. "The shy engineer types make wonderful husbands. They need us to improve their image."

Matchmaker, another dot.com, is a national business, and refines its California search area to the San Jose locale. A quick trawl through the men looking for women who have posted themselves on this particular site reflects the cultural diversity of the Valley.

It can't be presumed that all those people work in the tech industry, although there are pointers to the wealth of the population. A number of the men have submitted photographs showing them with cars, planes, at the door of luxury houses or against exotic backdrops. Some are pictured at work—in their cubicle, or at a desk. Some have posted intensely posed portraits, a few look out as obvious images off a scanner. At least half are in their late thirties or early forties, and are looking for a serious relationship. I look through the women seeking men. There are fewer status symbols in the pictures and more women, of all ages, seeking serious relationships with the opposite sex.

A few weeks later, I am standing in a store in downtown Saratoga. Two immaculately groomed women, late thirties or so, are discussing men, and the lack of suitable candidates. I recall Steve's performance and his approach to the female sex in the value-for-money sense. Those Macy's earrings. And then I hear the two standing close to me, speaking loud, and without a trace of candor: "You know," says one, "they have to be rich. I told that guy not to waste my time, I want holidays not day-trips."

The other concurs and lists the things she wants from clothes to jewelry, a few brand-names dropped in between. And then they both shake their heads and sigh.

"I don't know, it's just so hard to find a man these days, isn't it?"

WAYS OF BEING |

The logic of "running lean and mean" has permeated organizations, public and private, thereby increasing the number and variety of tasks many workers perform. Likewise, consumers face a dizzying array of choices involving such disparate products and services as financial instruments, utility providers and educational options for their children. These, too, increase the burden of daily chores and our sense that we are whizzing down a speedway, so that roadside attractions are but a blur. Furthermore, life in such a world becomes tightly coupled so that the effects of a single incident, like an accident on the freeway or a dead battery in the cell phone, can disrupt well-orchestrated plans and increase the sense that life is indeed out of control. Several effects combine to create the maelstrom—the flurry of rapidly occurring activities in lives already crowded with activities; and the constant looming threat of minor catastrophe.
—From "Living in the Eye of the Storm: Controlling the Maelstrom in Silicon Valley," by Dr. Chuck Darrah, Dr. Jan English-Lueck, and Dr. James Freeman, the Silicon Valley Cultures Project (SVCP), San Jose State University Anthropology Department

For the past nine years, Silicon Valley's lifestyle has been under the microscope. Anthropologists Chuck Darrah, Jan English-Lueck, and James Freeman have been studying the diversity of life in the region. The three have observed fourteen Silicon Valley families for 2,500 hours, and carried out over 1000 hours of in-depth interviews with another 170 people. They have had access to major corporations and institutions. Students from San Jose State have complemented this in the community, gathering thousands of shorter interviews and critical incidents. The results are posted on a website that makes the findings accessible not just to those taking part, but to internet users all over the world. In turn, Darrah and English-Lueck are now investigating the various Silicon offshoots, from India to Ireland.

Collaborators in the project are the Tech Museum of Innovation and the Institute for the Future in Menlo Park. Both institutions have an abiding interest in how technology is received by the public. The qualitative data provided by the Silicon Valley Cultures Project (SVCP) helps the Institute and others to identify cultural patterns, which can then be communicated to clients.

Silicon Valley is ideal for such an exacting investigation. "This region is a laboratory for research into high-technology industries due to its robust and varied industrial base, the use of information technologies, organizational innovations, and its broad cultural diversity," says the SVCP. Darrah and English-Lueck began the project in 1991. They conceived it as a "conceptual umbrella" under which classroom-based research could also be run. Darrah's educational anthropology background, and his colleague's psychological anthropology, helped to form the research, and the data helped to develop techniques of analysis. Those teenagers growing up in the Valley would turn the gaze on themselves and in turn be gazed upon.

I meet Darrah for coffee at the Blue Rock Shoot in downtown Saratoga. I'm interested in his own take on Silicon Valley. He's an old-timer. His family has lived in Mountain View since 1925. His grandfather built the house and true to form, its value has skyrocketed from around $5,000 to just short of $1 million in that time. Darrah smiles as he describes this phenomenon—"houses on steroids." But it was not an exponential rise. In the midst of the "maelstrom" comes a reminder that ten years is a long time in SiVa. In 1990, Silicon Valley some said was dead in economic terms. There was a real possibility that the tech and innovation nexus would shift elsewhere. The organization Joint Venture was formed as a direct response to those fears. The big question it asked was "How can we keep companies in the valley?"

But Darrah contends that the Valley's fortunes wax and wane. Even three years ago the feeling prevailed that the days of big money had gone. Then came the dot.coms. Stanford students would be into start-ups before finishing their MBAs. They made claims on a birthright—"a new BMW or Lexus every year." Hubris did not get a look in. New allegiances were made. "To kind of work rather than company." Networking was crucial. "You didn't know who was going to be boss." There was an inherent contradiction in working out of some region called "Silicon Valley," by defining its parameters as a technological and entrepreneurial zenith. The world was increasingly virtual and place became irrelevant. The world was turned on its head. It was OK not to succeed. "It was about 'I wouldn't have you because you haven't failed enough.'" Darrah is fascinated by this "ecosystem of failure," the mitigation of risk, the spin doctoring. As an ethnographer he observes this transient technoculture that holds diversity together; as someone living in the heart of Silicon Valley he is participant as well as observer.

Looking at things is central to the research carried out by Darrah and his colleagues. The Infomated household project was sparked by the findings of the Institute for the Future. "People who had five or more consumer information devices (ranging from pagers to computers) had a distinct profile from those who had less. They called this mysterious group infomateds." The researchers looked at how the devices were being used in house-holds and "in oblique ethnographic fashion, we explored their link to technology by examining how relationships were enacted using these devices." The data revealed "a fascinating juggling act."

As Nicholas Negroponte observed in his work *Being Digital,* 1995, "Computing is not about computers any more. It's about living." There was a new social order. Photographer Paul Mueller has been capturing these mores through the lives of a married couple in Silicon Valley. Scott and Cara France are both involved in start-ups. Mueller has charted aspects of the couple's lives both tech-related and otherwise. Cara at her gynecological exam. Scott talking to colleagues at a meeting. The couple exiting San Francisco airport, with Scott on a cell phone, and Cara on what looks like a cell phone. In fact she is scratching her ear. Scott stands on the beach at Pacifica. Cara ponders the fittings in their new home. Their pet cat mews as it peers down from the stairs.

Scott and Cara France, San Francisco Airport. Photo by Paul Mueller.

Mueller's two-year research project is based at Stanford University. Over the course of his work he tells me his take on the project has changed. From regarding Scott and Cara as a "Silicon Valley couple" and looking out for ways in which that manifested itself, he was now documenting them as a couple, who just happened to live in Silicon Valley. It was now reportage of people rather than concept.

Years ago, when I was at journalism college, we'd be sent out to find stories on notice boards. In the middle of the "for sales" and "wanteds," there would invariably be some gem of local newspaper interest. "House clearance, owner sailing the world." "Plants free—husband has extremely rare allergy." "One-eared toy bunny lost in park. Please help, child hasn't eaten for two days." It's a fascination that's never left me. Over in Woodside, I read the notice board outside a store and log the contents for August 29, 2000.

Help. Lost dog. We love her and miss her [and telephone number]

Woodside pony club—"Be there or be square."

Accommodation wanted: "Local resident would like to stay in the area. My rent went up, my wages have not. If you are interested in renting to a quiet, non-smoking female, please call."

Art exhibit, Palo Alto

Tipis, all sizes for sale

Help wanted $15 an hour (Notice in Spanish)

Internet users wanted $120 possible per hour

Hauling and clean-out offered

Landscaping

Pet sitting

Show saddle for sale $1500

Childcare provision (two notices)

Cleaning offered

Accommodation wanted by Stanford medic; a couple; tree worker.

Horse wanted

Dance classes

Fitness class

There's something oddly comforting about the ordinariness of these notices in one of the most affluent, and scenic, parts of Silicon Valley. And the fact that, with all other means of contact around, thumbtacks and paper work are still employed. These ads are not too dissimilar to those on notice boards outside the Valley. They continue to offer regular services—childcare, clearance, pet sitting, fitness and dance classes. They have the same appeals for help with work, accommodation, and lost pets. But sift further and two cultures emerge. Hispanic help wanted—$15 an hour. Internet users—$120 an hour. The plea for accommodation from a local person being priced out of the market. A few scraps of evidence. A multitude of stories.

Mike Cassidy is one of the best storytellers in Silicon Valley, a place dubbed "the biggest domestic news-story in the country" by a senior newsman at the *San Jose Mercury News*. For the past four years Cassidy's been writing a column. It's from an anthropological gaze that is wry and amusing, usually quirky, often technologically irreverent. The umbrella theme is: "It could only happen in Silicon Valley." Whatever the size of the NASDAQ, his reporting patch is hardly a dull one. And the uncertainties of the year 2000 are producing a feeding frenzy of human-interest stories.

I chat with Cassidy about reporting responsibilities. His career began in Chicago. Little surprise then that he has always been sensitive to the other side of Silicon Valley's economic boom. After over fourteen years of reporting in the area, he is less seduced than many by what it all stands for. The heart of the problem, he figures, is the lack of real community. "There's no real central place. San Jose is a sleepy town that has huge industry on the outskirts. A population that comes in and moves out means there's often a sense of disconnection. The community is created within a company."

And the hoary question of philanthropy in Silicon Valley? It was all to do with results and problem solving. "And homelessness isn't a problem that is obviously solvable."

Today, December 4, 2000, Cassidy's "Silicon Valley Dispatches" is a pithy piece on another closed-down business. Not a dot.com but the regular kind that existed before the Santa Clara Valley changed its name. Cassidy's story charts one more victim of escalating property prices. "I know. Another week. Another closing. If it's not a favorite bookstore, it's a classic hamburger joint, or a neighborhood bakery. And now a recycling yard." Cassidy is concerned not just with the loss of this business, but a way of doing business.

Thinking about the high-tech tsunami of Silicon Valley I am reminded of an incident a few years ago. I went to a showing of a film called *Koyaanisqatsi,* an American movie made in 1993 and directed by Godfrey Reggio. It's described in Halliwell's *Film Guide* as "a panoramic view of contemporary America without commentary or narrative." Its images are set to music by the minimalist composer Philip Glass. The edits crack an accelerating pace through technological change to the space race and beyond. This particular showing in London was accompanied by the original music, which, crucial for this story, was being played live on stage by the Philip Glass orchestra. The music started, the film began.

The crowd murmured. There was a fine hair in the projecting gate, wildly distracting the gaze from the image. Old technology. At first the hair moved and threatened to fall away. But then it was held fast as a trapped moth. The orchestra was still playing away, the conductor presumably oblivious. There was no way of telling him, alerting his gaze to the screen, of stopping the performance. If the film was halted for the gate to be cleaned, the music would be out of synch or everything would have to start over. So, for the whole of the film, the hair flickered and flinched, as the subject matter—unstoppable change—reached its climax with the orchestra all the while gathering momentum. At the end, some of the audience demanded a refund. Others, who got the irony, went home with an uncertain smile.

TRAINS AND PLANES AND SUVS |

Mid-October 2000 and I'm journeying on Amtrak's Pacific coast
train from Seattle to San Jose. The full stretch reaches down to Los
Angeles, in a two-day journey from the northernmost redwoods to
Hollywood. I'd come in at a touch under 1,000 miles.

The Coast Starlight seemed a neatly anachronistic way to return
from interviewing the tech pioneer and computer collector,
Nathan Myhrvold. Only as the train rumbles southward do I realize that I am traveling a silicon route—a stretch from the terrain
of Microsoft to the heartland of computer history in the Santa
Clara Valley.

It's a twenty-four-hour ride, which feels like a cruise after the
outbound flight and its usual stop-start delay. In his classic work
on the impact of the railroad on time and space, Shivelbusch had
described the trauma of the earliest high-speed rides. Today, glid-
ing serenely into Silicon Valley, I feel I should be wearing a bonnet
and stays and reading Henry James's latest saga.

For the final leg, from Oakland to San Jose, the journey takes
on a new sense of discovery as I re-explore those locations previ-
ously seen only from the freeways. The backs of sprawling residential areas, the industrial plant, the metal struts and girders that

support a nation. An underpinning that seems visible only from the pioneering routes carved out by the railroad.

There is more wetland than I imagined. Alviso comes into view and deserves full attention from the train window, as much for its gentle marshscape as the role of rail travel in the town's decline.

Spanish missionaries used Alviso as a landing stage. It was then called Embarcadero de Santa Clara, and changed its name after Ignacio Alviso established a ranch on the land. One hundred and fifty years ago it was a thriving port, aspiring to greatness as a main shipping route across the Bay to San Francisco. In 1864, the railway linked San Jose to San Francisco and cut into the port's passenger and cargo trade. The train won over sea travel, and now the freeway competes with the train.

Alviso is protected as a national Historical Place and Country Park, just a few miles from downtown San Jose and the burgeoning city of Milpitas.

Pulling in to San Jose's station is a different experience from coming off a freeway signed with place-names that evoke little more than tech centers, companies, and associations—Stanford University, Palo Alto, Mountain View, San Jose . . .

Like most things in Silicon Valley, San Jose's airport started small. Sixteen acres of Santa Clara Valley farmland leased from the City of San Jose in 1945. James M. Nissen and a group of businessman built a 1,900-foot runway, a hangar, and an office building. The first flights began a year later. Nissen became airport manager and retired as Director of Aviation only in 1975.

To meet the growing numbers of passengers, the terminal building, built in 1965 to handle 124,000 a year, was expanded in 1969, 1970, 1971, and 1983. In 1984, with a service to Canada, it was renamed San Jose International Airport. The Silicon Valley phenomenon was underway.

In 1987, the airport was handling 5.7 million passengers a year. By 1998, 10.5 million—a growth of 84 percent. In 1999, it was the thirty-fifth busiest airport in North America. In that year it shipped or received 13,760,515 pounds of mail. Its taxicab operations recorded 391,719 trips. There were just over 7,000 airport parking spaces. In 1999, there were 294,739 takeoffs and landings—808 a day. Another major expansion was begun, with all the associated infrastructure.

Such infrastructure means, in the main, roads. An extension to BART—the Bay Area Rapid Transport—from San Francisco down to San Jose is expected to ease the traffic problem but will take time to construct. After the Loma Prieta earthquake in 1989, a major section of Highway 280 was rebuilt. The 101 and the 680 on the other side of the Bay took diverted traffic. Ten years later all three routes are heavily congested. Links into Silicon Valley from other areas that are becoming regular commuter routes, such as the notoriously dangerous 17 from Santa Cruz to San Jose, are the only through routes. Even with all roads open, the rush hour in Silicon Valley starts before 6 A.M. and begins again at 3 P.M. In some places the traffic seems never to abate all day.

In Silicon Valley, development favors utilizing former sites while cautiously exploring new areas. In the fall of 2000, the ongoing controversy of Cisco Systems' major development plan for Coyote Valley in San Jose took another confident stride. The project is set to bring around 20,000 new workers into the city, with obvious knock-ons for housing and transportation in the area. It will open up the area known as the South Valley, spreading further the geographical range and economic impact of Silicon Valley.

The *Silicon Valley 2010* report notes that the region creates jobs much faster than housing, and traditional interpretation of the use of space from material evidence alone points to an increasing relationship between home and work bases—how do people move between one and the other. Telecommuting is not as pervasive as might be assumed, and high housing costs also factor the distances traveled to get to a work place. The report notes that the development of residential communities on agricultural and other undeveloped lands threatens the Bay Area's ecosystems and biodiversity. "Growing outward is also fiscally imprudent because it costs taxpayers more to provide new infrastructure than to redevelop land where there is existing capacity."

Despite the two-person fast lane on freeways, the other lanes remain congested—and traffic problems are increasing. On the one hand, single-person use of cars is regarded as an abuse of the environment; on the other hand it is an expression of individual freedom in the premier car-oriented society. It is also a necessity if the driver works long or uncertain hours, the former being part of the Silicon Valley culture. What is regarded as selfish driving— usually involving the use of cell phones—is regularly castigated in the pages of the *San Jose Mercury News*. I return to road rage later in this book.

If "Pompeii" happened on the freeway, the evidence would be difficult to decipher, given the number of collectable vehicles— old low-rider Chevrolets, convertibles, and other classics of America's love affair with the wheel—in the same lanes as Porsches, Ferraris and the new king-of-the-road, the Sports Utility Vehicle, or SUV. This tarmac-munching monster reminds me of the "off-road" transportation that became fashionable in Britain during the 1980s for the suburban school-run. Fleets of vehicles that could withstand most of what the earth could pitch at them are being used on super-smooth highways to pick up dry-cleaning, children, the pooch from the veterinarians. The anti-SUV fervor in the press scales new heights when cell phones are also involved. Drivers complain that the size of the SUV impairs their view ahead on the freeways. Even so, they are endemic in Silicon Valley, a place where gas costs more than most places in America.

In 1999, the Porsche Club of America reported its highest increase in membership—more than doubled—was in the Golden Gate Region of the United States. That's the club serving the San Francisco Bay area. It has 1600 members, who drive a variety of Porsches, from classic 911s and 912s to the top of the range vehicles that cost on the high side of five figures. A little to the south, the Loma Prieta regional chapter serves the Santa Cruz area, and also picks up membership from Silicon Valley.

Reasons for being in the club range from wanting simply to improve driving skills, to having a yen to push the car as far as it was built to go. Or not even built—many members enjoy modifications to their cars that make them sportier, increase their power, and improve safety at high speed. Members autocross their vehicles around a coned track at speed, go on Time Trials around a race circuit with other Porsches; they take part in rallies and concourses, and hang out at swap meets, admiring each other's vehicles.

One chilly November weekend saw me getting behind the wheel of a friend's thirty-three-year-old 912. It was one of those events that should have gung-ho, macho, boys and toys written all over it. In reality it was anything but and leaves me hooked. For a start a number of the drivers are female and reach times touching or tipping the men. Myself excluded. These PCA events ride roughshod over the more usual perception of the historic German marque and its owners. Pretension doesn't get a look in. Instead there is practical advice, not least on safety, first-timer and improver instruction, friendly chat over picnic lunches, and good-hearted badinage over the PA system. The system is work, rest, and play. Drivers work while others run. They work in the timing trailer, or on the track, or flagging. And there's a certain ritual in everyone mucking in to pick up the hundreds of cones at the end of the day.

The first event was Golden Gate Region's, at Dublin, on the grounds of a former jail turned police training headquarters. It was the last GGR Autocross of the season, and some eighty Porsches turned out. 944s, 911s, 914s, 912s . . . The chapter's newsletter is called *The Nugget,* a name that ties in the Golden Gate and the technological gold rush that sent the sales of high-end cars soaring. The editor ponders this month the relationship between car model numbers and digital clock timings. This is, after all, a Silicon Valley stronghold. The timed laps over, some Porsches purr on with fun runs until sundown.

Next day's event, run by Loma Prieta, is held further south, at a airfield near the ocean at Marina. A bigger track, signs requesting cars give way to aircraft, and straight runs without those cushioning practice laps. Two very different courses. But both require utter concentration, grim determination—and a sense of humor. Smile, as a knocked-about orange cone get trapped and trailed under your new $100,000 Porsche! Grin as you spin your classic 912!

THE TECH

My Dear Madam

I enclose cards for my last two parties of this season. I hope you intend
to patronise the "Silver Lady." She is to appear in new dresses and
decorations . . .
—Excerpt from a letter sent by Charles Babbage to Ada Lovelace on
June 10, 1835. Lovelace Byron Deposit, Bodleian Library, Oxford
University, no. 168, Letter no. 35. Extracts used by permission of
Laurence Pollinger Limited and the Earl of Lytton.

April 1, 2000, Skinner's Auction rooms on Main Street, Bolton, a
few miles from Boston, Massachusetts. It's a bright morning in
rural New England, and the saleroom car park is already packed.
I'm thinking that every techie for miles around is after the items of
computer history on offer—a piece of the ENIAC and other items
linked to its design. The ENIAC—Electronic Numerical Integra-
tor and Computer—was a calculating machine developed by
J. Presper Eckert and his colleague John Mauchly to meet the
needs of the military for improved ballistics formulae. The sale is
in effect a technological narrative through time to Eckert's very
own tool-kit. The Eckert material comes from his widow, who
approached auctioneer George Glastis after her husband's death.

She had wondered what to do with some special things left in the attic.

Once inside the saleroom I am faced not with a sea of techies, but regular folks eating breakfast and wearing "Music Box Society" badges. One woman is doing a needlepoint of a rose garden. For a moment I think I am in the wrong place, then I look more closely at the catalog and find this "Science and Technology" auction also features mechanical music. In fact hundreds of music boxes, automata, and other novelty items are on sale—from a musical monkey trio to a rocking sailing ship, and an early twentieth-century German speaking picture book. The morning progresses through a string of singing birds, slot machines, amputation equipment, and wooden telephones—a bunch of which are sold for less than a high-end cell phone. As the mechanics of these artifacts become both more complex and also more recognizably modern, I am reminded of an intriguing segue into early computer history—Charles Babbage's collection of automata, and his invitation to Ada Lovelace to come see his dancing "silver lady."

The crowd starts to thin, estate cars are loaded up with mechanical wonders, and I get to thinking about the likely people here for the ENIAC. Over homemade cake and coffee, I start talking to Peter Eckstein, who has also figured out that I am not a fully paid-up member of the Music Box Society. He is here for reasons of historic interest—he writes academic papers on early computing. But he has a personal interest too. While he's bidding for the documents, he is also hankering after the tool-kit. In 1992, he interviewed Presper Eckert, and remembered seeing the tool-kit at his home. It's estimated in the catalog at $500 to $700, and Peter is cautiously optimistic. "Let's just see how it goes."

It follows that the early computer lots come at the end of the afternoon, after some technological star-turns—"Mills' one-cent

Wizard fortune teller"; a "Saratoga Sweepstakes Coin-operated horserace game"; and the "Globe Coin-Operated Grip Test Muscle Developer" (just don't argue with the person who paid $4,500 for it). And on past the various sewing machines, radios, Geiger counter, electric motors, generators. The catalog cover is lot 521, a splendid sign from the 1920s, promoting Electrical Prosperity Week. It shows Columbia throwing a switch and bears the slogan: "Do it Electrically." Just before the ENIAC comes a demonstration laser outfit, a ray gun used by the late Professor Arthur Schawlow of the physics department at Stanford University. Also up was his prototype "laser eraser" from 1967—designed as a means of erasing typewritten and manuscript mistakes. The words sledgehammer and nut come to mind.

Lot 524 is a Keuffel and Esser Model 4083–3 Log-Log Duplex Vector Slide Rule, inscribed on the underside with J. Presper Eckert Jr., and used by him during the development of the ENIAC. Lot 525 is a pocket tool-kit, by D. Peres, Germany, from the 1930s, which is believed to have been used by Eckert while he worked on the ENIAC. Lot 526 is three early descriptive booklets on the UNIVAC, one with a sales letter of 1948–1949, and a magnetic tape—a unitape—from the UNIVAC. Glastris notes the significance: "These booklets represent the earliest marketing of the computer industry."

And then, with the saleroom left to a handful of people, up comes the Eckert material. Lot 527 is an archive of documents relating to J. Presper Eckert's professional life—including papers regarding his appointment and resignation from the Moore School, the assignment of patents, the formation of the Eckert-Mauchly Computer Corporation, drafts and texts of articles, reports and speeches, court cases, and memorabilia. Lot 528 is another collection of memorabilia—Eckert's Univac Co. photo ID tag, his Franklin Institute medal and report, diplomas from the University of Pennsylvania, his National Medal of Science, a 1960s drafting set, three early radios, text books, and a film about UNIVAC.

The catalog shows Presper Eckert pictured with a ring counter from the ENIAC similar to the one offered as Lot 529: "ENIAC: A Decade Ring Counter, the black steel chassis with twenty-seven (of twenty-eight) vacuum tubes, ten indicator light apertures, two male plugs on the exterior and one outlet inside, various wires, busses and connections, and labeled on back inscribed 'Front Office J. P. Eckert,' wd. 45in, and a schematic disgraphic from the Moore School of Electrical Engineering, dated November 20, 1943, for the Accumulator Decade Unit." The estimate is $8000–$12,000.

The slide rule is sold for $3000. I watch Peter Eckstein as the tool-kit advances up the scale, past the estimate. I am willing him to get it. He stops bidding and the hammer goes down at $475. The UNIVAC booklets go for $2000 and it becomes clear that there are some real collectors here. When the ENIAC ring counter comes up as the last lot of the day, the tension is pretty remarkable. Bidding is fierce. It sells for $70,000.

The Eckert documents have been bought by Jeremy Norman, a collector and dealer in rare books and manuscripts in the history of science and technology who is already building a major collection on Eckert.

The Eckert papers will join his unique collection of material about Univac I, serial number 1, which he owned prior to the Eckert sale. "The two collections form a perfect match since Eckert did not retain much about Univac I in his archive."

He later emails me with some interesting findings. They call to mind an anonymous tenet of archaeology: "Absence of evidence is not evidence of absence." The papers are valuable not only for the written information itself, but as evidence of those documents that Eckert thought worthy of saving—or that survived over fifty years. Norman notes:

I have done some preliminary sorting of the material. There are many gaps. Most of what he saved was drafts of his own writings and things to do with awards and honors, etc. of which he received a great many. There are documents from his life before Eniac but none of the notebooks for Eniac or Univac. My guess is that these could be in Delaware with the Sperry Rand archives.

Some of the most interesting material from my perspective include autograph and typescript drafts of his efforts to rebut the republication of the Goldstine and Neumann report on the theory of the IAS computer when it appeared in Datamation in the early '60s. He knew that this document and von Neumann's 1945 draft threatened his patent, and even before the patent was granted he stated the history as he understood it. Eckert seemed to feel that von Neumann had been his nemesis, since von Neumann deliberately attempted to prevent anyone patenting the general theoretical principles of electronic computers. Were it not for von Neumann the Eniac patent might have stood up. Eckert never mentioned Atanasoff—possibly he did not understand how influential Atasanoff had been on Mauchly. In any case I view this Eckert—von Neumann drama as the central theme of Eckert's life.

Jeremy Norman's collection is now housed north of San Francisco in Marin County. It's become so extensive, he's publishing a bibliography of his personal library on the history of computing and telecommunications. It's a fascinating area of joint technologies. "My collection of computer literature begins in the seventeenth century and extends to the founding of ARPA.net in 1969." He also has a parallel collection on the history of telecommunications. "The histories of the two subjects are now more interrelated than ever with the convergence of media on the internet."

Peter Eckstein goes back to Michigan empty-handed, but glad to have watched pieces of computer history go under the hammer.

He emails me to say that he was able to check some data and so it was far from a wasted trip.

Auctioneer George Glastris is delighted with the day. He says the material made the sale unique. Although this was a special case—with the pieces having such a distinct provenance—this live auction sale marked a new area of specialization. It was the beginning of technology as marketable— "but only the finest and earliest pieces—the preconsumer computers." Skinner's advertising on the web had attracted e-bids, though the big players would have sent their agents in person. I start to make discrete inquiries about the identity of the ENIAC buyer. Six months later I would finally meet him.

In terms of archaeology, what was special about the Eckert material was the provenance. The knowledge that the artifacts could be directly related to such a monumental part of computer history upped the stakes in terms of marketing, desirability—and inevitably value in financial terms. As the sales on the eBay auction site have shown, there's a growing market for old computers. But what has to be decided is where "old" becomes "interesting." It's often a matter of taste.

A few years ago, I was walking in the rain past a dumpster in a residential street in London. I noticed what looked like a painting face-down on some old bits of broken furniture. Curious, I turned it over. It wasn't a brilliant piece of art, more like the work of an enthusiastic amateur. But I felt sad that this was now heading for a sodden garbage heap, so I plucked it from its obscurity and put it under a hedgerow till I could pick it up later. As I lifted it out, I noticed it was sitting on a pile of paintings, all on hardboard and in various subjects. The rain had eased off, and so I turned each of the paintings around and made a dumpster-gallery of them. I figured someone might take a fancy to one of them. When I came back later that afternoon, every one of them had gone. I salvaged the last from under the hedgerow and walked away wondering if I had liberated them to an art appreciator with a few blank walls, or given a fast buck to someone who would sell them on. It's also possible that the artist—who had gone out that morning rest assured that work related to the most traumatic time in their life had at last been got rid of—had returned in horror and gone in search of a bonfire.

The story illustrates not only the way of taste, but attachment and detachment to and from objects. A thing can be defunct and yet valuable if it holds memories. The appreciation of J. Presper Eckert's tool-kit was, for me, enhanced by Peter Eckstein's story of seeing it in the home. For auctioneer houses, the provenance does not need to be so personal—a letter or academic documentation is more the norm. Sometimes a photograph of the object will be displayed with it. In New York, I went to a charity auction of some earrings made for the late Diana, Princess of Wales. The person who bought them, a storeowner from Texas, told me he liked the idea of having something connected to Diana. He thought he'd display the jewelry in his store on special occasions. But his interest wasn't exclusive. He also collected things connected to Elvis Presley. The point I am making is that the "thing" itself doesn't have one meaning making it "valuable," one association that makes it equally precious to everyone.

In nine times out of ten, what someone wants to dispose of, someone else will want. And if more people want it, the price goes up. That's the origin of trade and its dynamic since prehistory. In Europe, for example, deals were done for Neolithic hand axes made of stone that were not local to an area. That's a simplification of what is in effect a very complex process involving distances, labor, and trade routes and relations, but put as simply as that, once desire is created, an emotional response kicks in that is not necessarily "rational." Personal associations and stories are part of the "value" of an object—witness the sales of estates from the Duke of Windsor and Mrs. Simpson to that of Marilyn Monroe. A simple hairbrush is imbued with a something "extra" relative to the emotional response of the would-be purchaser. That's simple economics and why auctions of what is basically second-hand clothing and sundry chattels work so successfully.

In such a new market as early computers, the playing field is still being leveled. Most cases, computers consigned to dumpsters are left where they are, apart from the possibility of them being recycled as parts. But changes are happening quickly, and museum collections, such as that at Intel Corporation and The Computer History Museum Center, are responding by trying to produce an assemblage of oral history, handwritten testimony, and artifact. The object comes to the collection wrapped in a meaning that is in a contemporary cultural context. Even two years later, in tech terms, new questions may be posed of the same object, particularly if cross-cultures are involved. In 1999, I tried to replace the floppy disc carry case I'd bought in the United States three years before. "Floppy discs?" said an incredulous New York shop assistant, "do you still use those?" In Britain we sure did.

This book is about rates of change in meanings. Here's an example from an archaeological standpoint. In 1809, a young nobleman set out on a grand tour of Europe from his country home, Westport House, on the west coast of Ireland. He was the Marquis of Sligo, and on his travels was accompanied by a close friend. Together, they visited the classical sites of Greece, which he had read about in his family library. At one of the most famous sites, Mycenae, in the Peloponnese in mainland Greece, and mentioned by Homer, he took a fancy to a pair of 3,500-year-old carved columns. They adorned the entrance to a curious building that was shaped like a beehive, thought to be a treasury or a tomb. Sligo, captivated by the romance of Homeric epic in which Mycenae featured, was determined to return from the site with the two columns, together with sundry other pieces of carved and interesting-looking masonry. They would be impressive souvenirs of his trip.

To ensure the cargo returned to Ireland safely, Sligo sought reliable seamen for his ship—but he slipped up. A few years later, an admiralty court at the Old Bailey in London heard how Sligo had procured his extra sailors. They had been bribed with drink, brought on board ship and hidden, and finally abandoned on a Greek island when Sligo panicked. To compound the felony, the men were Royal Naval seamen, and England at that time was at war with France. One of the men died somewhere in the Mediterranean; two others returned to Britain to tell the authorities. Sligo's mother put up such an impassioned plea for her son that the judge fell in love and married her. The nobleman, whose defense was that he was a young man caught up with the magic of "the Grand Tour," was found guilty and jailed in Newgate Prison in London for six months. His crime was nothing to do with removal of antiquities, but the manner in which he had chosen to ship them.

The columns had reached Ireland on Sligo's initial triumphant return from his travels, but were left neglected in a basement at Westport House for one hundred years. By that time archaeology had marched on as a discipline, museums were established, excavations mounted—and knowledge disseminated. It was the "modern" world, and the general public was more aware of what was held to be of value and interest, culturally and fiscally. A descendant of the Marquis came across the columns and, realizing they might be of importance historically, donated them to the British Museum. The columns now form a principal part of the display of Bronze Age, or preclassical, Greek artifacts. So let us consider the parts of this story again. The masonry was presumably valued in its original state and purpose, 3500 years ago. It fell into disrepair and was "lost," was revived by the interest of a nobleman as a souvenir of his grand tour, became cargo, put in storage, named in court evidence—though not contentious in its own right—forgotten about again, revived once more—and finally displayed with value as significant archaeological artifact.

The case in point is the changing nature of "value" over time. The columns had a biography, they became history, and now form part of the story of ancient Greece. There are two links here with the material culture of computers. The first is that pieces of computer history have a story, whatever their age; either the items have a personal attachment to the owner, or they are part of the story of computing, even if they are just off the production line. The rate of change apparent in Silicon Valley only makes this case more interesting. Things are redundant, obsolete, cranky, old, and suddenly collectible, all within a short space of time. Shorter certainly than the one hundred years it took the columns from Mycenae to be recognized and prized for their value to archaeology, which, even at the time of Sligo's travels, was an area barely discernible from antiquarian collecting.

And the second link is this. Sligo's traveling companion in Greece was Lord Byron, father of Ada Lovelace who found her own place in the Computer History Hall of Fame.

At Chaco Canyon in New Mexico, the National Park Service has been vexed by the problem of modern votive offerings. By these, I mean items such as pseudo–Native American crafts, bundles of sage-brush, feathers, crystals, and other objects such as tiny metal "Dungeons and Dragons" figurines. National Park Service Rangers, watching people practicing behavior—chanting, dancing, praying—in certain parts of the prehistoric site—might describe it as "ritual," and the objects used in this activity become "ritual objects" by association. Taken out of their context, they return to being craft goods, bundles of sage, crystals, and so on. But when considered as part of the bigger picture, they have a meaning that is both personal to the people engaging with the objects at that time and place, and communal in the broader scope of the way people use a prehistoric site. Such objects are now collected, accessioned into the objects associated with the site, and regarded as "archaeological." The problem has arisen because of the sheer quantity of objects gathered at one time, which peaked in the late 1980s, and the sensitivities of the other groups using the site who have their own ritual practices and beliefs. For each group, there is a concept of "value" that is not necessarily shared by the other groups, or individuals. It's all relative, and that is what makes collecting interesting.

An hour out of Silicon Valley in downtown San Francisco, the Museum of Modern Art in 2000 staged a major show of objects from the 1960s and 1970s. This was hippie art, appreciated by a whole new audience. Or several audiences. Those who remembered using, wearing, or making the objects now on display in lit, glazed cabinets beheld a value that may have been nostalgic, evocative or derogatory, depending on their view. Those confronted by these objects for the first time would have formed a different perspective, based on aesthetics and appreciation of the craftwork—if they liked the embroidered clothing or could admire the carved, velvet-finished throne, even if they could not imagine living with it. They may also have had a personal recollection of something their parent wore or owned, or had an album cover or re-release on CD, which came from the same era of association by ornament. Some may have found the quaint rainbows and flowers laughable. Others found a place for such recent art an insult to the institution. But there it is, conserved, displayed, publicized, and visited. After thirty years, the art of a major phenomenon is canonized, becomes a movement, and takes its place in the discussion of ascribed value.

How to forecast what to keep and what to discard is part of the business of collection and curation; "value" is in a relationship with rarity, and yet the fact that millions of computers exist in the world does not stop computer museums and computer collectors from holding on to examples of the most commonly made. The BBC Micro, a machine with widespread distribution in the U.K.'s schools, was so common that few thought to hold on to it when it was superseded. It was old technology. And yet at least one leading computer collector I know is avidly in search of one. But that brings us to another point. He is American; the BBC was made for the British market. Here we have another issue of "value"—cultural displacement, which means one man's or woman's cast-off is another's quaint curio from another locale. Remember, as L. P. Hartley wrote: the past is a foreign country, they do things differently there—but the foreign is just as useful and intriguing a resource for the collector of old computers.

Which brings me to the "collectors" themselves. My observation suggests a number of distinct groups—the individuals who have a passion for old technology and who may, or may not, have a background in programming or other engineering; the individuals who are in it for the money and see computers as part of the "new, new thing" with racing values; those who find old technology aesthetically appealing and find the idea of a brown-housed, green display more fun, perhaps more ironic than their tangerine iMac; and those whose life is so much part of the Silicon Valley dynamic that collecting old machines, and having the funds to be able to do so, is as important and valid to them as having a trunkful of old badges, baseball hats, and prom photographs. The computer is a part of their personal material culture as much as it is the material culture of a distinct region of northern California, and its offshoots across the United States and the world.

Collectors may be open about their interest, meeting at regular computer hardware auctions, or at gatherings such as the pioneering Vintage Computer Festival, started in 1997 by Sellam Ismail, an experienced programmer from California. Its first European meeting in 2000 attracted around 100 collectors, but this does not fully illustrate the significant network of enthusiasts who discuss computers and trade over the net. Ismail plans to turn his 1200 computers, plus collection of manuals, discs, tapes, and ephemera, into a public access resource, where aspiring engineers can learn on old models, in the manner of a would-be young mechanic learning the nuts and bolts on a Model T Ford. Apart from the hardware and tangibles, Ismail's work illustrates a practical side to the collection of old machines and the know-how to run them. When data is locked into a machine that cannot be run, the aged software programs can generally be resurrected and the data retrieved. It is like the Rosetta Stone being deciphered, with vintage software becoming the language to make dead machines and data come back to life.

May, 2000. In room 132 of the New Bodleian Library at Oxford, I am reading some of the correspondence between Ada Lovelace and Charles Babbage. The letters were important communications between two massively intense and brilliant scientists, beginning a dialogue. On June 10, 1835, Babbage writes enclosing cards for the last two parties of the season. "I hope you intend to patronise the 'Silver Lady.' She is to appear in new dresses and decorations . . ."—a reference here to Babbage's fondness for automata.

There are letters discussing scientific problems, and glimpses of the obsessive nature of the pursuit. On November 29, 1839, Babbage writes an apology for the late reply: "I have even more than usual been occupied by the Engine. . . ." The historical importance of these to computer history is plain and I'll get back to these later, but looking at the pile of papers in Ada's hand, there was something else at play. I was struck not by the content, but the very idea of holding in my hand the paper she had held, scribbling out not just letters to Babbage and Augustus de Morgan, the mathematician she wrote to on a prolific basis, but the scratched black fountain-pen work of the algebraic formulae, the triangles, curves, and numbers.

All meant nothing to me in terms of mathematics, but the passion with which Ada Lovelace had filled pages, the ink leaking through both sides, was palpable. If I hadn't known this was Ada's work, I would have regarded the pages as a curiosity of the Victorian mind; if I hadn't known its age, then I would still have appreciated the passion of the pursuit. But knowing the authorship of the letters, the bundle of notations, the quest for satisfactory answers, I saw these as documents that linked objects to person. Ultimately, archaeology explores that relationship. "Value" is a movable feast; its reconstruction requires imagination, a malleable mind that is open to the possibility that the oddest, ugliest, least-interesting, all-round deadliest object to a twenty-first-century Western-canon-schooled mindset could rapidly become the coolest, most scintillating, charming artifact, worthy of curating, cataloging, and putting on display in a museum, and/or paying serious money to own.

I switch on my laptop, and to my complete amazement, Ada's image comes into view. She sits impassively on my screen, trapped there by electrons like Grace Hopper's infamous "bug." It turns out that I had somehow "selected" her as my screen startup image from a slide-show held on my computer. Of all possible permutations and key-strokes for this nontechie to make, I had somehow moved her from the gallery into center stage at this most auspicious moment. Her portrait gazing out at me, as I input the contents of her handwritten letters into a computer with which she was connected, by a technological chain of causation. She is the ghost in the machine.

THE EARLY TECHNOLOGY TRAIL |

Humans, of course, have a memory strongly connected with smells, and as soon as I walked into the computer museum, the smell hit me in the head, and I remembered the old days in which I spent a lot of time around these old "computing engines."
—Stan Mazor, an Intel pioneer, November 2000.

Here's a test of archaeological interpretation. The discovery of a few plastic discs marked "Intel" scattered on the ground within sight of known major financial institutions, the venture capital powerhouses on the Sand Hill Road. Spatial pattern of the finds suggests random placement. Nearby are some strange receptacles made of metal and glass-fiber, holding one or two people facing downhill; and a man on a podium whose garb is so dissimilar to the tee-shirts and sportswear around him, it can only be supposed he is some kind of deity. This is obviously a votive center and sacrificial arena.

But while human sacrifice might be one of the activities associated with the extremist work ethic of the Valley, this is an arena for fun. It allows the techies to have fun with technology, while helping fundraise for community projects. As an MC yells encouragement, a motley crew of boxcar enthusiasts set off down the hill. In their guise of cigar-shaped projectiles, science-fiction creatures, and laptops on wheels, they represent high-tech corporations, dot.coms, schools, and youth projects. No stock options on offer here. Just free Frisbees, coffee, and muffins for the crowd.

Like a laptop next to an ENIAC, The Computer Museum History Center is dwarfed by the giant hangar of the historic NASA Ames research institution at Moffett Field in Mountain View. But not for long. A major scheme over the next few years will convert Hangar 1 into NASA's California Air and Space Center—and a much-enlarged History Center will be right next door. It's designed to be a world-class institution. It also develops the idea of computer history as a resource, and one that is set smack in the heart of Silicon Valley, putting it within its own geographical context. The visitor will reach the center by driving through the technological hub, and emerge back into it. Here, for the most part, past and present will collide.

The comprehensive tech collection at Boston's Science Museum performs the same function on the East Coast, drawing its context from the innovations of Route 128. Apart from such science museums, for which computers are part of a broader history, those institutions dedicated to new technology have displays that feature a familiar array stretching back over the past century and a half. Some have examples of the forerunners to computers. A few Heath Robinson-type machines make an appearance. An example of an early Cray—the world's first supercomputer—is a popular well-known name. It is also an example of function and design in combo, the circular seat shape being the most efficient way of wiring the machine.

There will be a few commercial mainframes, minicomputers and early PCs, Macintoshs, Apples, together with attendant peripherals. Punch cards and the machines that run them are still recent enough to be quaint and yet within recent memory, prompting another aspect of an archaeological approach, artifacts given "voice" by narrative.

The Computer Museum History Center is a nonprofit body founded in 1996. Its mission is "to preserve and present for posterity the artifacts and stories of the information age." At November 2000, its holdings included more than 3,000 artifacts, 2,000 films and videotapes, 5000 photographs, and 2,000 linear feet of cataloged documentation and gigabytes of software. Documentation ranges from advertisements to programming manuals. Curator Dag Spicer shows me one of the most endearing artifacts—a "Kitchen Computer" made by Honeywell, which featured as the year's luxury item on the front of a Neiman-Marcus catalog. The machine was designed to help the busy housewife, by storing her recipes and helping her quantify ingredients. Dag doesn't think any were sold, but the model is an interesting concept. Importantly it illustrates how people perceived a role for the computer in society.

In 1961, Robert Heinlein's *Stranger in a Strange Land* described a culinary experience of a similar nature: "Service was by non-android serving machines, directed by controls at Miriam's end of the table. The food was excellent, and so far as Jim could tell, none of it was syntho."

The Museum acknowledges itself to play "a unique role in the history of the computing revolution and its worldwide impact on the human experience." The role of individuals in this process is crucial, as those who owned, or even played a role in the design of, early machines donate much of the material. As at Intel, the artifacts can generally be traced back to a source, and through that process the stories, retold. Technical lectures and talks are a vital part of the Museum's work.

John Toole, the Museum's CEO, is a former White House tech advisor. He is sensitive to the place of the early engineers in the great scheme of the Silicon Valley. He tells me that for the retired

John Toole and Dag Spicer, The Computer History Museum Center. Photo courtesy Computer History Museum.

tech worker, the chance of describing his role in the development of the nascent technology can be emotionally cathartic. He adds: "One man was moved to tears, and explained that this was the first opportunity he'd had to tell his story."

There is an annual ceremony for Fellows of the Center, those people recognized for their contribution to computer history. And some retired workers get involved as volunteers who work on collections projects, on artifacts, in the archives, or in administration. They are working on objects which are personally familiar. The Center produces a quarterly publication, *CORE*. Corporations and individual supporters help to finance the Center. It receives a range of donations—from hardware and software to audio recordings and ephemera—and given the qualities of machines produced, particularly personal computers, the potential material base is enormous.

To help with the process of choosing what to collect, and what has no value to this Center—although it may have value in another sense—the Center has developed specific criteria for donations. It will consider the object if:

The item is unique. This includes prototypes, rare machines produced in low production runs; odd products that never made it to market; or homemade items or documents from someone who went on to contribute in a significant way.

The item was mass-produced but has a low serial number. By "low" is generally meant something between the serial numbers 1 and 10.

The item was the first of its kind or is more than thirty years old. Donations of artifacts and materials from the early 1940s and '50s are especially worthy, although the collection begins in the nineteenth century.

The product was a great idea ("ahead of its time") but never sold or sold poorly.

Anything by a seminal inventor, for example, Seymour Cray.

The History Center has a Collections Committee, which meets at least once a week to evaluate offers of donations, using detailed descriptions sent, faxed, or emailed to the Center. It fields initial inquiries, but not items sent simply on spec. The donors of items accepted are responsible for getting them to the site, including shipping costs.

The Center also specifies what it doesn't want. "It's difficult for us to turn people away when they have taken the time to contact us about a particular item. Sadly, we must do this when the item in question is something the History Center already has or has decided does not meet the History Center's Collections criteria."

As of November 2000, some of the items no longer accepted included the following: IBM PC, IBM PC Jr, Commodore PET, Commodore 64, Commodore VIC-20, Apple II (+/c/e) TI 99/4, Timex Sinclair. "These items were made in large quantities and the History Center has representative samples of them already." The Center supports the recycling of unwanted machines.

The smaller-scale Computer Museum of America, on the campus of Coleman College in La Mesa, California, accepts all donations of computer-related materials "except for defective monitors." Working computers not used by the museum are refurbished and donated to schools and other nonprofit organizations. The CMA also has archive and research materials, and established a Hall of Fame to honor those making major achievements in the computer history field.

As computer history interest grows, individuals and organizations are setting up collections in other locations. In America, as more tech hubs emerge outside the East and West Coast corridors, it seems that before too long, it will be possible to visit a range—however limited—of computer history at any drivable distance. On the internet, the Vintage Computer Festival and Classic Computing sites flag up numerous user-groups with an interest in preserving specific machines and associated material.

The Computer Museum History Center is part of a Silicon Valley tech.trail, which stretches from the corporation museums, such as Intel, to the significant Tech Museum of Innovation—affectionately known as "the Tech"—in San Jose. The trail includes the headquarters of household names and their space-time relationship, which is their evolution across Silicon Valley. In San Jose, the expanding Cisco buildings are little short of a form of monumental corporate architecture in style and scale. The development of a tech company's research headquarters as a "campus" has spawned significant landmarks, such as the Sun campus, which incorporates historical motifs in a mission-style in keeping with the area's architectural heritage.

Low-key in scale but highly significant historically are the founding locations of the significant companies. These include the garages associated with the early days of Apple and Hewlett Packard. In these buildings the first key developments were made. In Palo Alto, the namesake company bought the Hewlett-Packard garage, with house attached, in late 2000—for more than $1 million.

Over a few modest years, a tech company can chart its history in geographical location and the size of its parking lot. Archaeologists would surely find this a more reassuring piece of evidence than a house with numerous bedrooms and parking for thirty-five cars. And there may be more unusual signs of prosperity and expansion. Steven Levy, in his 1994 afterword to *Insanely Great—The life and times of the Macintosh: The computer that changed everything,* describes returning to the Apple headquarters at Cupertino after Steve Jobs's departure.

"Apple's 'campus' was now unrecognizable from the modest complex of the Jobs era. The faux adobe buildings on Bandley were abandoned: Apple now occupied a phalanx of fresh-off-the-assembly-line junior skyscrapers . . . scattered on the lawn were huge sculptural representations of the icons one finds on the Macintosh desktop: cursor arrow, watch and so on. A tangible tribute to the success of the Mac team's do-or-die gambit."

By 2000, Jobs is back at Apple's headquarters. The company with the inspired address of "Infinite Loop" attracts enthusiasts from all over the world. There is no on-site museum; Apple's historical archive was donated to Stanford University. Apple's familiar rainbow trademark sign can still be seen on car bumpers and on the side of monitors. But its corporate sign is now updated to reflect the new color ways of the iMac era.

In the exclusive area of Woodside, home to Oracle's Larry Ellison and Intel's Gordon Moore, Buck's is a cultural icon that thinks it's an American diner. It's a place that marks time in two ways—the historic high-tech deals done over breakfast, and the assemblage of things hanging from, attached to, gracing and playfully disgracing its walls. A Russian cosmonaut suit dangles from the ceiling. There's a one-of-kind catch and release fly swatter—"for the sensitive, compassionate, holistic, caring person of the '90s." A sign from a nuclear fall-out shelter is close by displays of pens, thermometers, silicon chips and wafers, ribbons and braids, swords, a flying fish, a broken John McEnroe tennis racquet, the skin of an anaconda, and a Buck Rogers mural. And that's just for starters. Follow that visual smorgasbord with tidbits of fascinating conversation involving venture capitalists and tech entrepreneurs. If these walls could speak, this would be an oral history book of Silicon Valley.

As it is, owner Jamis MacNiven, who runs Buck's with his wife, regards it as a museum. A homegrown museum of jurassic technology. "It is devoted to irony," he says. As an example, he provides the captions for photographs on display and then advises: "It's up to you to believe that, of course." It provides a perfect example of displaced meaning. Is that really a picture of one of Iceland's premier politicians? Does it indeed relate to the narwhal tusk? It's next to it. So it could be. But Jamis has a twinkle in his eye.

What is entirely plausible, however, is Buck's reputation. Its diners number the great and the good of Silicon Valley, who take breakfast early and conclude their multimillion-dollar deals over coffee and muffins. Netscape was founded here, Yahoo! was turned down twice. The Buck's menu is a newsletter, the web page a gallery of fun and fame. Jamis used to be an artist in New York

City. "When I moved in here, it was a white box," he says, casting his eyes around the walls. Now he maintains his creativity by dreaming up ideas for the walls and writing a film-script about Silicon Valley.

And once a year, Jamis dons zebra-skin shorts, or something equally arresting, and takes the microphone as Master of Ceremonies at the Boxcar Derby.

Jamis MacNiven, Buck's Diner, Woodside.

COMPUTER FIELDWORK |

The passage of time often constitutes a kind of selection committee; objects of beauty stand a better chance of being preserved than ugly ones. But in many cases—such as archaeological finds—we know there was no selection committee. Ugly objects in their own age survive side-by-side with beautiful ones; and yet we find beauty in them all.

—John Fowles, *The Aristos*

On a Sunday afternoon, the old General Motors factory in Oakland is an international bazaar. At a plant where Durant and Star automobiles came off the production lines, this landmark has new life, and the stalls inside reflect the diversities of Bay Area culture. It's a hot day, and the car park is heaving with vehicles, windows wound down, pumping out various world beats. Up a concrete ramp and into the glazed upper floors, and I'm shown another culture set—crossing not so much geographical boundaries, as temporal and technological ones.

This is Sellam Ismail's vintage computer warehouse. It takes some getting used to. Once my eyes get adjusted to the low light, I can make out stacks of boxes, computer monitors, keyboards, and cables, all heading out of sight. There are around 1200 different

Sellam Ismail, Oakland, January 2000.

computers here in a technological A to Z that reaches from the Altair to the ZX80. There's a modest, and innovative, home computer kit, colorfully packaged like a children's game. Apple Macintosh Classics sit with Commodore PETs. Machines from the once-massive Digital Equipment Corporation gaze out to other giants, a couple of mainframes swathed in polythene. The more I look, the more appears.

Sellam's collection began when he was still at school. His first computer was a Mattel Aquarius—a simple machine made by the toy manufacturer best known for Barbie, but also one on which Sellam learned to program.

"I decided I wanted to get an Apple II computer and so in order to fund the purchase I sold my beloved Aquarius to a boy younger than me—I believe he was 9 or 10, I was 14. At the time I was a bit sad to see it go, but I figured it was good because I was about

$50 closer to owning the Apple II. However, now I look back on it and regret selling it. I realize it is as much a part of my personal history as my photographs and other memorabilia I did keep. It helped lay the foundation for my current life in computers."

Sellam still has the program listings of the games and things he wrote on the Aquarius. "Those are tucked away in a box somewhere but as they were printed on thermal paper, which is prone to fading over time, I have only a short time left to transcribe those programs to some other more permanent medium before they are lost forever. But those listings really are the soul of the work that I did on that computer."

Eventually Sellam acquired another Aquarius, and most of the peripherals he had with it originally. He is still searching for the printer and the cassette recorder. "But having the program listings and being able to replicate the work that I did sixteen years ago really brings back the experience, more so than just the hardware itself."

Sellam's point is highly significant. Archaeologists attempt to decipher intentions and manner of use from survivable things, when other vital data—organic remains, or sounds and action— may be missing. The skulls of early modern hominids can indicate brain size, but long gone is the soft matter, the tongue and the vocal chords, which suggest the power, the ability, of speech.

He reminds me that hardware is just the shell of the vehicle, and without the software it is lifeless. It provides Sellam with a reminder of the experiences he had with it. "But still having the software allows me to make the experience alive and real again. It is the soul of the machine. It almost sounds like a person, doesn't it?" This informs his work on recovering "lost" data from elderly machines.

Still in his twenties, Sellam is utterly driven by his passion for early computers; even in the middle of moving hundredweights of equipment to a new home, not least keeping tabs on manuals and other ephemera, he is still accepting more donations. Old computers never die . . . they end up at the warehouse.

His compulsion to collect began in the mid-'80s. It was sparked by regrets he felt after selling his first computer. "I didn't have the heart to let go of the machines that I had spent so much time with and learned so much on."

In 1986 he acquired a Commodore and a Texas Instruments model, foreign to him as he'd spent so much time in the Apple realm. At this time they were not just artifacts, but for use. In 1989 came some machines from the very early '80s. "This gave me my first exposure to the architecture of the first generation machines of the late '70s, although I didn't realize it at the time."

These computers came out of an all-girls' school in a small mountain town northeast of Sacramento. He was attending a computer interfacing class at the local community college and one of the students was a teacher at the girls' school. The teacher rescued the computers from the trash as the school was upgrading to new models, and told his students to sign up if they were interested in having one. Sellam was lucky, and it was an event that he reckons marked the beginning of his big-time collecting.

"I ended up later on taking two other computer systems that other students took but soon realized they couldn't do anything useful with them as they were outmoded. These other students offered the computers to me because I'd actually taken the time to write a text adventure game for the machine, which I passed out copies of in class to those who also got one of the machines. They figured I would be best able to do something with them. The truth is I didn't have room for them but I just couldn't stand the thought of them simply being thrown out, so I accepted them."

Sellam was still living at home, where his mother wanted to know why he was holding on to old machines. "She'd implore me to get rid of the ones I wasn't using on a regular basis." Sellam's justification was that nobody was holding onto them anymore and they might never be seen again. He began to get an idea to open his own computer museum.

"In the early '90s I acquired an Apple Lisa from my then boss, which I thought was really cool. And then maybe a year later I acquired about fifteen different computers from a flea market. I remember how excited I was when I came upon them, but I can't recall exactly why I was excited. I don't quite remember if I was into collecting at that point or was excited because here were a bunch of computers that I lusted after ten years before but couldn't afford, and now I could have them for $5 each. I must have been interested in old computers and their history back then but I guess whatever interest I had in computer history then pales in comparison to the enthusiasm I now have, and it's hard for me to remember it.

"My collecting basically ended there for a while, since I was consumed with my job. But then in 1997 I joined the Classic Computers mailing list. It was only then that I came to realize that there were others in the world who shared my passion of saving old computers from the trash. It was then that I began to collect in earnest. I started to frequent the local flea markets and thrift stores in search of computers. I started to meet other local collectors and a loose local coalition began to form."

Within a couple of months, he began to plan the first Vintage Computer Festival. "I wanted to do something with my collection, but the most obvious thing, making a 'computer museum' on the web, was already a stale idea. I wanted to do something unique that had more impact. I discussed a convention for computer collectors on the Classic Computers mailing list and it met with a lot of interest. By the summer of 1997 the plans for the first VCF were starting to get laid out. And I was collecting like crazy.

"I didn't quite know where I was headed with the VCF at that point, only that I was very excited about doing it. I was looking to establish a 'place' for myself in this fledgling computer collecting community, which I recognized was fairly large and growing. My reasons for collecting were still more personal, wanting to go out and search for odd and interesting computers that I had never seen before and learn a bit about them."

The passion became an addiction. "I eventually started to formulate the idea that what I was doing was getting bigger than myself. I was amassing so many computers at such a quickening pace that my collection was growing huge and I no longer had time to give any one computer any attention. I was more interested in acquiring as many machines as possible before they disappeared for good. I was also addicted to the thrill of finding new computers.

"I realized my collection was too large to be considered merely a personal collection. I started to describe my collection as an open resource, available to anyone that wanted to explore in it. A lot of this was propelled by the guilt I felt for hoarding all these computers I was collecting. I just didn't feel it was right that I should be acquiring all these computers and then just storing them away. They needed to be in the hands of people who actually wanted to do something with them. And I'd always been a sharing type, so it was natural."

Sellam spoke of his dream to have people run and work on the machines at a central meeting place—a potential community center for hackers, nerds, and geeks. "It would be a communal storage area, where I would sublet space to other collectors. We'd have workbenches and tools set up. It would eventually be the home of a computer collecting and homebrew club that I was thinking of starting, something that would harken back to the days of the Homebrew Computer Club."

He sees it also as a place to set up some educational programs for disadvantaged inner-city children. "It would be a place where they could learn contemporary computer science and electronics but using old computers that could be dissected and easily understood as the teaching tools."

Sellam told me other plans include producing short computer history videos to be broadcast off the VCF website, as well as a portable "museum" of computing artifacts and presentations at local schools. "More than anything, I hope that in fifty or a hundred years or more, people will appreciate the effort I went through to assemble this collection so that they can study computer history with the benefit of a huge snapshot of it being taken and preserved at a time when it was still possible to do so. Everybody has to leave some legacy, and this will be at least one of mine. That will be my greatest reward."

What makes Sellam's collection so interesting is that attention to detail which makes all these machines "lived-in." When he has acquired computers adorned with stickers, inscribed with felt-pen or paint, or even have a name and number gouged with a knife, he has kept them intact.

There is no restoration involved. These machines are truly state-of-the-art in that they have come straight from cubicles, or garages or studies or bedrooms. In most cases there is no history to the owner or what they were used for. There is no log-book, and such is the disposability of outdated technology, no need for service records for these personal machines. I hunt around for more personalization, and find initials. I am reminded of the way early antiquarians would carve their initials in ancient monuments in Egypt or Greece. A mark of possession, which also serves as a monitor of movement around sites. At what point does this act of vandalism become quaint and collectable in its own right—and does it ever revert to being vandalism? Of course, where computers are concerned, many of the marks are for security. Entering larger computer corporations in Silicon Valley, such as Intel, I had to hand over my laptop so its number could be recorded.

The items in Sellam's warehouse are intriguingly anonymous in the main. We talk about the importance of having a trace to a previous owner. But then Sellam reminds me about security. Those who used their computers for letters and financial details, even if they found a way to wipe the hard disc, may not want to be identified. In the same way, his software expertise is used by companies who have information locked into a computer that they can no longer read. The traces are still left on hard drives or software discs that are coded and, within short years, incomprehensible. The reverse is also intriguing—new software that emulates the old, so making the latest computer run like a model from the 1980s.

That aspect of retro computer technology is significant, and Sellam already lends out machines for film and advertising purposes, and helps lawyers with issues of patents and copyright. "The consulting work with the law firms and TV production came about by chance, but that is something I plan to keep up. It brings in a lot of money, and pays for the rent. My eventual organization will be very much centered on continuing to provide these types of firms with materials for research and so on, as it is the most immediate and realizable form of income for something that has not yet quite struck the imagination of the mainstream yet. I figure we're still a good five to ten-years away from the general public being interested enough in computer history that it becomes a self-supporting endeavor."

In the fall of 2000, the U.S. clothing store, Banana Republic, ran an ad campaign in which the models were photographed using adding machines with paper-tape. The stylists employing techno-irony figured that their target audience would find these objects "new" and interesting. This is in contrast to the sugar-gum color and clear acrylic computers of the twenty-first century—witness Apple's lead with the iBook, iMac, and the Cube—which is futurist cool. It figures that if clothing harking back to the 1970s can be complemented by cars and home furnishings, the technology of that period—from TVs on chrome legs in veneer cabinets, to book-sized calculators—can't be far behind. Analog—whisper the word—is suddenly chic.

Wired, in San Francisco, ran a major photographic feature of items from The Computer Museum History Center at Mountain View. The photographer, Todd Eberle, used the images in a whole show in New York.

If style magazines are already seeing the potential of old hardware, how far will those teens weaned on Silicon Valley in the 1990s take their aesthetic sensibilities? Watching a TV show from the 1980s, I could hardly believe the brick that passed for a mobile phone—one still, I should add, being used in a car but with the benefit of inducing the weariness of the driver, as much as the driver behind. In the late 1980s, working on a national newspaper in Britain, I was issued with a similar brick when reporting on an open-air concert in London's Docklands. The only way I could get myself heard by the copy-taker at the other end—an extinct species now but there were no modems in those days—was by jamming myself under a seat with the "mobile" and yelling down it. "I can't hear you," screamed the copy-taker. "That's because I'm at a rock concert!"—"A what?!"—"A rock . . ." and so it went on until the battery packed up a few minutes later.

Maintaining the historical theme it may not be long before museums display computers that were used for writing a particular document. An award-winning novel, say, or a major film-script. It would be like seeing the pen used to sign a contract or a declaration, or a quill used by a writer. With the advent of virtual signatures over the internet, and the intangibility of e-contracts, an Amstrad used to belt out a million-seller, or a Powerbook on which an Emmy-award winning series was drafted, would provide a palpable link with the particular history of ideas.

Such a link returns us to the notion of personalized objects. In this case it's a creative response mediated through a machine. I am loathe to part with the Apple LC11 on which I wrote my doctoral dissertation. It's pure nostalgia on my part, but I built a relationship with that machine over three years of my life. And I had acquired it second-hand from someone else at Oxford who bought it for her thesis. When I carried it away, she even said she felt quite suddenly sad to see a piece of her past going out the door. Although wiped of her files, the electrons, one figured, still vibrated with her folders and files.

I find it difficult to be unsentimental about machines, particularly those used to form words, which is probably why this non-techie is writing this book about computers. As keyboards become smaller and tech objects become, in theory, more intimate, they also become less so. Do those who first wrote on old-fashioned typewriters also miss the physicality of that writing experience? Sentences were pounded out, often through layers of carbon paper. Sometimes, carried away by a passionate piece of prose, or facing an imminent newsroom deadline, I hit so hard I tore into the paper and left holes, paper dust, and a reverse that could be read like Braille.

Taking this a stage further—and perhaps too far—there is also the nitty-gritty of other stuff left on machines, the molecular-level traces of human use: the gross in the machine. Coffee and sandwich debris were favorites in my old newsroom, and the remains of

"Pop-tarts" and single cheese slices would surely be present in geek-household ranks. I am reminded of Douglas Coupland's 1995 classic, *Microserfs,* in which a pair of computer programmers who haven't seen a fellow coder for days go shopping for "flat foods" to slide under his door. "We slid Kraft singles, Premium Plus Crackers, Pop-Tarts, grape leather, and Freezie Pops in to him. . . ." It would be a fun piece of archaeological science—to analyze the detritus of computer usage, to decipher the food and the other organic remains left on the keyboard and underneath, where no one sees. In years to come, this would be archaeological data, in the way specialists can find traces of cabbage and milk in 5,000-year-old ceramic pots, and build up a picture of the prehistoric diet. Evidencing further back in time, archaeological analysis reveals traces of blood and butchery marks on stone blades, and the organic gloss of scything on the earliest agricultural implements.

To get some flavor for Sellam's archaeological discoveries, I joined him for a collection of donated ephemera near San Francisco. Fred Cisin was leaving his premises in Berkeley and had magazines, manuals, and other stuff to donate to Sellam's cause. Pile after pile was heaped into Sellam's car. He showed me the haul; an array of documentation from the 1970s and 1980s. It would join the pile to be cataloged. For now it is squeezed into the trunk of Sellam's car.

After that we head off to a place called Weirdstuff, an electronic hobbyist's dream site in which the stacks are not as large as in Sellam's warehouse, but they contain bits and pieces of a more contemporary feel. Sellam shows me machines and parts of machines he has, but at present he couldn't find, or get to in his collection. I start to get an idea of the obsessive nature of collecting, the impossibility of drawing a line because of the range of things around the interesting earlier machines—the manuals, the various models, the components, the prototypes, the marketing materials, the bits and pieces that make up the assemblage.

Sellam heads off to a promising corner. With an expert eye, he wades in among the machines. The salesman, used to it, ignores him. Sellam suddenly spots something. Inching my way through a tight silicon alley in pursuit, I visualize him as an archaeologist, his head peering into an ancient portal, thinking through the best way to extract the evidence. I expect a landslide of gray plastic, or a crash or two, or at the very least a groan of not being able quite to reach the elusive machine. But Sellam's done this so many times before. The arch-collector brings to the surface something now made special by the very reason of its being desired. He releases his quarry—a machine he already has one version of, "but not this version." What comes next is a reel of numbers and letters. Baffled, I nod in agreement that this is worth buying for a couple of bucks. It seems cheap at the price, but Sellam sees the potential and thus it becomes, in this context, invaluable. The computer joins the manuals in the car. I see that moving Sellam's collection is like painting the Forth Road Bridge, or its U.S. equivalent.

His antenna up, Sellam is anxious to show me another hunting ground. We head off down the freeway and come to Mike Quinn Electronics in Oakland. It's another excavation site, this time with a slice of technological history intact. I look at the floor, with its multitude of wires and bits of chips and snaking cables and odd metal connections, and realize that I am standing in an excavation site. I could photograph and plan the floor.

I suggest that Sellam and I excavate a computer—strip it down to its components and trace them back to a source. He selects an old Apple for the job. It's a basic machine that was once new, boxed, and no doubt much loved and admired for its speed and high-tech accreditations. Before that it was designed, prototyped, assembled, unveiled, marketed and sat at the cutting-edge of technology. I pay five dollars for my stake in computer archaeology.

Quinn's was pivotal in the development of early microcomputer companies. It was a place not just for parts and pieces of parts, but where hobbyists could hear of each other and trade ideas, part of the fun days of the West Coast Computer Fayre, and the "Homebrew" meetings at the Stanford Accelerator. The role of such hobbyists is crucial to the personal computing story. As computer historian Paul Ceruzzi notes of that key period, there were two forces at work—semiconductor engineers developing ever more powerful microprocessors, and the users of time-sharing systems, who were rooting for public access. Were it not for the enthusiasts, Ceruzzi asserts, the two forces in personal computing might have crossed without converging: "Hobbyists, at that moment, were willing to do the work needed to make microprocessor systems practical."

The names of companies that spawned out of Quinn's—Godbout Electronics, later known as CompuPro, and Morrow—are barely known outside the world of computer history but are highly significant in the evolution of the technology. Quinn's is also believed to have played a hand in promoting the growth of Northstar Computers, Processor Technology, and IMSAI, all mid-to-late '70s microcomputer companies that were on the cutting edge of the hobbyist computer explosion.

In their way, too, hobbyists and enthusiasts helped develop archaeology. They traveled to sites, carrying out fieldwork that, despite being unsupervised and actively discouraged today, at least brought the idea of archaeology into the public domain. This interest also helped fund projects and brought in volunteers to take part in digs, field surveys, and carry out work in museums.

Early summer, 2000, and I'm driving down the Pacific coast with John Lawson, senior sound engineer at MGM Studios in Los Angeles. We turn off at Malibu, and head for the hills, the Malibu Hills familiar to movie stars and those who love the ocean view and environment. John has invited me to look at his collection of Digital Equipment Corporation computers. It's something of a close call, as John is leaving for a new life and job in "Bollywood"—the flourishing Indian film world. He's a friend of Sellam's but his collection is not going upstate to Oakland, nor to Mountain View—but crossing halfway round the world to Europe. One of Germany's leading computer collectors, Hans Franke, is taking on the machines, manuals, books, and other ephemera. But first, John has to pack it all up and get it shipped out there.

We reach the wooden house high up in the hills. Inside, DEC equipment is ranged around every wall; there are piles of books, bits of hardware, and all manner of fascinating stuff. John shows me a number of metal canisters containing NASA film of various missions. He got it as part of a computer trade at a swap-meet. Just as fascinating to me is John's spectacular life-swap, not least the transportation of the computer gear across the earth. In picturing the movement of the DEC computers from the port at Oakland across oceans and safe haven in Germany, I begin to play the "Pompeii" game. Well, not so much "Pompeii" as "Ulu Burun."

Around 3,500 years ago a ship sank off what is now the coast of Turkey. The shipwreck became famous in archaeology not just for its cargo, and its fine state of preservation, but for the methods by which journey of that cargo could be recreated. A battery of 1980s scientific methods including lead isotope analysis were able to determine the provenance of such goods as ox-hide copper ingots, and to sketch out complex trade routes around the Mediterranean of Bronze Age Europe. I was thinking about it in terms of Lawson's cargo—if the cargo was lost en route in the Pacific or Atlantic, or the North Sea, what would archaeologists make of it? Crates of heavy technical equipment, bearing the name DEC—Digital Equipment Corporation—which was originally made in the East

Coast of America, but in transit from the West Coast and on its way to an address in Germany. Lost would be the story of the collection process—the amassing of the computers from places not just on the East Coast but anywhere DEC machines had been sold to, or ended up via collectors. The personal histories of all of the computers would be lost, with the supposition perhaps that the machines were bound for use as computers by engineers or programmers somewhere else.

Just up the coast, at beautiful Santa Barbara, John introduces me to another computer enthusiast, Marvin Johnston. "I can't resist donations," he says, and sure enough, his collection has taken over the family house, garden, outhouses, garage—and old car.

Marvin Johnston, Santa Barbara, May 2000.

Machines that can't be plugged in, inside a car that can't be driven. As I leave, Marvin is telling me about possibly annexing a caravan.

Parke Meek describes himself as "a natural-born collector." I come across his store among the coffee shops in Main Street, Santa Monica, a few miles from Hollywood. It's a little hard to walk on by the window on this particular technological journey. The display features a van der Graaf generator and a model of Maria, the robot from the classic sci-fi film, *Metropolis*. Parke's store is actually a prop shop, serving the film and television industry. He was part of the Eames design team. Salvage yards provided much of the materials in Parke's early days—bits of electronic gear, coils, transistors, generators—but no computers. Parke doesn't find them interesting—yet. But he still has a website.

A film prop created and owned by IMSAI veteran and successor, Todd Fischer, was a big hit at the third Vintage Computer Festival. It is the computer at the center of the 1983 thriller, *War Games*. Todd was a consultant on the film, which introduced the concept of "computer hacking" to the wider world. The fate of mankind rests in the hands of a Seattle teenager, played by Matthew Broderick, who accidentally taps into the Defense Department's tactical computer and starts a countdown to World War III. The film has a cult following, an interest segueing neatly into the internet age with a string of dedicated websites offering sound and picture clips. For vintage computer enthusiasts, the film's up there with *2001: A Space Odyssey*. Early technology on screen includes an IMSAI—arguably the most successful clone of the Altair kit computer—and early IBM machines. The film's "tactical computer" WOPPER was made not in the Valley, but at a film studio at Borehamwood, England.

Todd had a front-row seat in computer history, as one of the band of pioneers at the legendary meetings of the Homebrew Club. Todd meets me at a hotel bar in Berkeley. He's patiently hanging on while I naively attempt to negotiate the rush-hour traffic from Silicon Valley without a printed-off Yahoo! map. As I recover with a cold beer I ask him for a picture of those fabled gatherings at the Stanford Linear Accelerator. "Well, you would go to the meeting with this air of anticipation." Todd says. "There would be quorums in one corner of the room, people would be talking about 8008s, 6502s and Z80s, or the latest thing in *Byte* magazine." The gatherings were once a month, on Wednesdays. Sometimes there would be 30 people there, sometimes 130.

The meetings were managed, but ideas were circulated in an atmosphere of camaraderie and free-flow of data. After the main business there was more fun outside the meeting, in the parking lot of the nearby Safeway grocery store. "There'd be six or eight, or fifteen vehicles," Todd says, "and we'd be swapping computer parts by flashlight." He laughs: "I had Woz round the back of my van once!"

Before computers, Todd had a career as a "techie" in the music business—he toured with Uriah Heep for three years, including their 1973 tour of Japan (and is the voice announcing the band on their "LIVE 1973" album), and gigged for the Doobie Brothers, Sly Stone, Santana, and Janis Joplin, among others. His move into computers came at a providential time. He was part of the Bay Area cultural mix that produced revolutionary art and music—celebrated in 1999 at San Francisco Museum of Modern Art—while also fostering the hobbyists. They used their expertise to develop gadgets that would one day change the world—and they had a ball doing it. "It was a golden era for the Bay area, " says Todd. "We were all hungry for chips. We'd all go round to Mike Quinn Electronics."

PROFILE OF A COLLECTOR |

Nathan Myhrvold bounds toward me like an archaeologist who's just unlocked a secret city. Not too far off the mark. Myhrvold started the research laboratory at Microsoft and helped create the stuff of legends.

Myhrvold joined Microsoft in 1986, when it acquired Dynamical Systems, a company he founded. He collaborated with Bill Gates on "The Road Ahead." Today he also heads up another company he set up, Intellectual Ventures, down the road from Microsoft, in Bellevue, Seattle. He's worked with Stephen Hawking at Cambridge and has a doctorate in theoretical and mathematical physics from Princeton.

And what we are talking about today is something that really, really gets him excited. His collection of things.

I'd been intrigued to meet Myhrvold since finding out he was the buyer of the ENIAC part at Skinner's sale in Boston. The scientist who loves pieces of history. Myhrvold's passion is calculating machines. Well, and typewriters. And dinosaurs. And eccentric pieces of technology. We sweep through the lobby of his offices and I try to keep up with the profusion of elderly keyboards and wondrous devices on display. I am distracted by the piece of dinosaur leg that stands where most other offices would have a potted plant.

Nathan Myhrvold, computer collector, Seattle.

Myhrvold reminds me that not only does he collect dinosaurs, he digs for them. He funds excavations in the desert and relishes getting his hands dirty in the process.

In a garage out back is a king-of-the-road Hummer, and a top-of-the-range sports car. For once in the tech world, a garage is just a garage. We move to Myhrvold's main collection depot, a warehouse down the road. To call it storehouse understates its collector's zeal for finding not just the unusual but the significant.

Chronology ranges from fossilized dinosaur eggs and other sundry bones to computer parts that are actually recognizable. The oldest artifacts are Babylonian cuneiform tablets, used for calculation. There is a set of "Napier's bones," an intriguing device invented by John Napier in the early seventeenth century. In fact there are three sets. "They were sticks used to do calculation," he explains as I reveal a black hole where my math synapses should fizz.

They are part of the mathematical collection, which also includes slide rules of every known size and shape. These are both baffling and beautiful. Carefully calibrated by hand and quite exquisite. One example would have been in use 150 years ago, at the time Babbage was working on his Analytical Engine, which was a precursor to the ENIAC. This brings us to an extraordinary project that Myhrvold is financing. In the manner of a philanthropist bringing Leonardo da Vinci's creations to life, he is funding the reconstruction of Babbage's calculating machine. It will be to the Victorian mathematician's design and proves to be a vast undertaking.

Engineers are working as closely as they can to Babbage's original intentions. They are using brass, bronze, iron, and mild steel, fashioned as much as possible to the same engineering tolerance. The work is being carried out with the Science Museum in London. There will be two machines. One will go on display in the museum. The other will enter Myhrvold's collection.

On the shelves there are two Enigma machines. These fabled code devices helped to decide the outcome of World War II. A box, some parts, and engineering brilliance. The box and parts are tangible, the brilliance invisible but essential to the whole. I reflect that there is an analogy here with just about every piece of technology, from early retouched flint tools to microprocessors.

The "thing" is the external world, the shell, the skull of the brain's processing.

Myhrvold has a selective array of later computer technology. A CM2 supercomputer, five Crays and pieces of core memory. There are around 100 personal computers. "I did spend a period actively scouting for machines that were being junked." Now the grapevine and eBay alerts him to objects coming up for sale.

And of course in the midst of the collection is the ENIAC part, which brings us to talk about objects with meanings attached. And indeed, Myhrvold's collection includes hardware of which he is fond for personal reasons—their association with the early days of Microsoft. They are both a part of his history and a universal computer heritage.

The objects are stacked in an order that seems known only to the enthusiast and his two assistants Joan and Dawn. It seems random, but most of the things are in transit. These objects will be housed in a new home being built for Myhrvold near Seattle. It has been specifically designed to display the artifacts to best advantage. Although he says he buys for himself, Myhrvold has thought about putting his collection on display. A gallery at home seems a median between warehouse and museum.

I try to get some idea of Myhrvold's motivation and it is always connected with the very idea of connection. A joining-of-the-dots in the story of technology that helps him to place his work, and that of other modern technologists, in a wider context. "Individuals are not thinking of being part of the whole thing, part of a grand scheme," he says. "The technology industry doesn't respect its past. No one thinks of saving old stuff."

For Myhrvold the paleontology enthusiast, technology goes way back, further than the cuneiform tablets. He learned how to flint knapp, to chip flakes to make stone tools.

At the other extreme of time, another of Myhrvold's passions is "The Long Now," the innovative time-keeping project devised by computer scientist Danny Hillis with another early tech hero, Stewart Brand. Myhrvold is helping to fund it. In his office at the warehouse he has a tungsten sphere, a hand-sized but immensely dense object that will form the pendulum of the centerpiece "clock."

Heading deep into the collection, Myhrvold has a surprise for me. It's a Tesla coil, a circus trick of early experimentation with electricity. His assistant turns off the lights. Myhrvold flips a switch. And although I know that there will be a crack, a sizzle, and a lightning flash, I still manage to scream. The lights come on and the smell of ozone lingers in the air.

Myhrvold disappears into his own studio space with the photographer, the Babbage-era slide rule, one of the Enigma machines, and a model *Tyrannosaurus rex* with the trade-mark name of Stan.

I wander around his extensive book collection, which ranges from architecture and art to whale watching, woodworking, travel, and anthropology. I am hardly surprised to find books on magic tricks.

On a worktop, I also find something a little out of kilter with the collection, but obviously meaningful. A small bottle of unfiltered extra virgin olive oil from Baena in Spain. With an accessionist's eye I am already noting its bottle number—246915—and other details of its vintage. 1999–2000 Nunez de Prado. I ponder on its place in the collection. Meaningful association with another object? The only bottle that survived a cataclysm?

I ask Nathan Myhrvold. He gives me what in England we call "an old-fashioned look." "I bought it," he says, "to cook with."

RECYCLING MEMORY |

After the visit to the spring the king conducted them to a prison in
which all the prisoners were bound with gold chains—for in Ethiopia
the rarest and most precious metal is bronze.
—Herodotus, *The Histories,* book III

Value is subjective. In the New World, conquistadors favored gold;
Aztecs feathers. The premise of this book is that computer development in Silicon Valley is just recent enough for a chain of
"value" to be clearly seen from engineer to manufacturer, salesman
to consumer, and back into the trade, post-redundancy, as part of a
collection.

In each case, the change in value is determined by a market
force, powered by the incessant drive for faster, smaller, sleeker,
most advanced, then cheaper and back to abandonment—whether
passed along the line to a less-demanding user, donated to charity
shop, or sold for a fraction of the "value" a year before. In terms of
the massive commercial mainframes, the scrap value is so small as
to make the statistics barely comprehensible.

Only where there is a veneer of nostalgia for its original function does value increase, making old computers collectable. And

then most often the biggest financial outlay is for haulage and shipping.

The frequent purchases by collectors such as Sellam Ismail—at swap meets, electronics surplus stores, via the internet, or at specialist sales—highlight the reduction in value in money terms. Multimillion-dollar computer equipment has a price tag of a few hundred dollars. The fate of the machine lies with the newly ascribed value and the collectors' market. If enthusiasts do not buy the computers intact, the machines are stripped down, parts are cleaned and reused, and the most valuable component, gold, recovered.

In some cases form dictates a different function—the use of server storage casing as furniture, as seen in Tom Jackiewicz's apartment in San Jose—and it remains to be seen what ingenious uses will be made of old handhelds and laptops.

Otherwise, the out-dated, clumpy, and/or out-paced computer represents a technological extinction. The machine as cutting-edge high-tech material is utterly obsolete. The enormous cost of research and development is invisible. Only the logo of such names as "DEC" or "IBM" or "Apple" remains as some indicator of previous value. Outside the world of the computer collector the hardware is redundant.

But an interesting hinterland is emerging between the "value" ascribed by the computer collector and that ascribed by the high technologist. Tony Cole is a businessman from Hayward, south of San Francisco, who sells what he calls "memorybilia." It's a neat way of describing his product—memory boards made into gift items. And not just any memory boards. These come from an early supercomputer, the Cray-1. "This Cray system is the granddaddy of them all," says Tony, whose interest in the Cray goes back to his childhood. Cole's machine was destined to be melted down and recycled for the five tons of copper and gold inside. Its provenance

was also historical, as it came from the nationally renowned
Lawrence Livermore Laboratory on the eastern edge of Silicon
Valley. Cole says the machine cost $19,000,000 when purchased
for the lab in the late 1970s. That colossal figure represented years
of research and development.

Cole bought it for $10,101.01. "A binary number!" he says.
After that he bought a Cray-2, Cray-3, and a Cray-4. "Then I
bought some from a salvage place, and I got a hold of Cray-YMP
and Cray-XMP. Those were very expensive because I bought
through a middleman. They usually up the prices by three times
the amount."

The original Cray-1 weighed thirty tons and required its own
electrical substation to run. Cole reckons the electricity bill must
have run to around $35,000 a month.

Cole markets his range over the web. Cray-1 and Cray-2 Core
Memory Boards and ECL Logic Boards are in Lucite and have serial
numbers, date code, and a dedication to "Seymour R. Cray." Each
plaque comes with a Certificate of Authenticity specific to the
piece encased in the plaque. The memory boards are $150; the
Cray-1 ECL Logic Board is $200.

Cole's customers generally come from within the industry or
have some association with it. Nathan Myhrvold bought several
boards for Christmas gifts. He told the *San Jose Mercury News:* "For
a certain class of nerd, it's a really nice thing to get."

Tony Cole takes me to see the guys at Hackett's recycling in San
Jose. Larry Hackett and Mark Levitt run an extraordinary empo-
rium of computer bits and pieces. It's a cross between an abattoir
and a trading post. And if you are a computer enthusiast, a candy
store.

Outside the warehouse, the hulks of computers are piled up in
bins. Multicolored cables contour and coil round each other in
dumpsters. Ten years ago, most of the stuff would have ended up as

landfill. Today the sheer volume of machines makes recycling a big issue. This is the place for machines that are beyond Goodwill or refurbishment for schools and overseas programs.

Sometimes Hackett's gets overstocked parts, but in the main these are outmoded computers brought in by individuals and companies. Occasionally items are left anonymously on the doorstep. Hackett's is a middleman operation. "We're proud to be helping the environment," says Larry.

And there's money to be made in recycled hardware. Not as much as one might imagine, as there are overheads. It's not enough to rip out chips and sell them on. They have to be cleaned and refurbished. "We pride ourselves on how close our used parts look to new," says Mark, as he walks me though the process.

The computer components are redistributed through a reciprocal agreement with other recycling firms. "We deal in the passive parts. No circuitry." Larry and Mark sell chips and boards. The memory boards are the kernel of the machine. By supplying the innovating techie, Hackett's is part of the development of the next round of new technology. There are customers far outside Silicon Valley. A website broadcasts details of the inventory. "There are hundreds of thousands of different part types, maybe millions," says Mark.

A disassembly line of workers pulls out a computer's vital organs. The parts are heated until the lead solder melts, then cleaned, refurbished, inspected. A young woman uses a toothbrush and magnifying glass to inspect the prongs of a chip. She lets Tony take a digital photograph. When I look at it later, I see she has personalized her workbench with family snapshots. They are visible under the plastic as she works.

Another Oriental woman is replacing the solder on the near-completed chips. It looks like a cooking process. She tweezers each

goddammit, England!
it's Asian

Recycling, with family photos visible. Photo by Tony Cole.

delicate object into flux, and delivers it to the molten solder. It sizzles. Then it is placed in a colander-type device while it sets hard. Other workers strip out the gold and copper wire, which sits shimmering in containers. It gets sent on to other specialist recyclers who deal in precious metals.

Recycling of materials, particularly metals, is nothing new. Archaeological science suggests metals were melted down and reused 3,500 years ago. The labor involved made all metals precious. Early technology required the movement of materials, such as tin and copper, around the Mediterranean. Values shifted but remained relative. According to Herodotus, born around 490 B.C.E., the Ethiopians prized copper as more valuable than gold at that time.

Over thousands of years, trade routes were exactingly established through skillful dealing and networking. An increasingly specialized workforce was engaged in extracting ore and smelting metal. This required knowledge of sources and the ability, in terms of economics and entrepreneurship, to take part in the transaction.

Spin forward to the year 2000, and the going rate for some recycled precious metals in Silicon Valley is measured in mere cents per pound.

So, in the middle of the gray and black of chips and boards in the Hackett's warehouse, there's a bin stuffed with pieces of gold. Tiny pieces. The gold wires are minute pieces from computers. Almost negligible. But such is the turnover that the bins fill quickly.

Mark grabs a handful of gold. It looks like a hoard from a Near Eastern tomb. I think of the excavation reports, such as one account from the royal tomb of Ur in Mesopotamia. In the chamber, archaeologists heard the tinkle of metal. They had disturbed minute pieces of gold decoration that was falling off the weave of decaying fabric. It had been worked into the cloth 5000 years before.

Rather like archaeological artifacts, each recycled item is inventoried with a tracking number. The items are stored in banks of containers in a stock room. When sold to a techie, they eventually return to their technological context. But taking them out of circulation for a time puts them somewhere else on the evolutionary path.

At the computer recyclers, memory is made tangible. Its containers range from "donuts" to motherboards. The place is a great example of Moore's Law in action. The Intel cofounder, Gordon Moore, famously predicted that in chip production the number of transistors would double every eighteen months. This memory-to-cost ratio is central to the SiVa dynamic.

It is also the place where "value" sets collide. The chips represent colossal numbers of man-hours in terms of R & D. And Hackett's processes millions of such components each year. But change is so rapid in the world of technology that even new parts are wildly undersold. In a regular electronics store a piece such as a video card for a computer may be on sale for $10—new—when it contains chips worth $20. Meanwhile, a 1970s "vintage" computer with a recycle scrap value of $1.50 may sell for $200 to a collector. In the meantime, parts that are still useful in technology terms, but are for some reason hard to find, gain a rarity value and up goes the market rate.

I notice some of the memory boards at Hackett's are pretty damaged. Mark points out where a part has been deliberately destroyed with a drill, or holes have been punched in the chips, to prevent reuse. This is, after all, Silicon Valley, and there's also a concern that the hours of research and development spent on chip design may fall into the hands of the opposition. People don't want to compete against other companies who have bought up their own unwanted chips.

And this presents another interesting analogy to archaeology. In some circumstances objects are regarded as having been ritually "killed" by being damaged. Pueblo pottery bowls found in graves may have a hole punched in the bottom. It takes them out of circulation and marks a change in their function. In Northern Europe, sites held to have been used for votive offerings frequently contain weapons that have been similarly "killed"—swords are bent or shields have a hole punched through them. This is not simply explainable as battle damage.

And in northwest Native American culture, the ceremonial "potlatch" symbolizes conspicuous consumption by elaborate feasting together with the destruction of precious decorative coppers. Often these are smashed through.

There are other leftovers from the process at Hackett's, the board part of the circuit boards. Sometimes these are refashioned into mouse mats or clipboards. Others become decorative art—shot through with a nail and attached to a wall.

I learn something else at Hackett's that epitomizes Silicon Valley culture. Across the road from the recyclers is a homeless hostel. And some of its community are regulars at Hackett's. Not for parts—but to sell computers. And where do they find them? In dumpsters all around the area. Outmoded junk, which companies haven't the time or the incentive to recycle themselves. A homeless person who may never have used a computer can make $1000 out of a single dumpster.

There's something pretty cannibalistic about the metal recycling process when it comes to computers. Copper ripped out of defunct machines or unwanted motherboards is turned into ingots, which, in their turn, get used to make the copper parts for other computers.

A few days later, I'm at Noranda Recycling in San Jose. It's a sampling plant for a major metal, mining, and resources company in Canada. The company takes a stage further the material that Hackett's retrieves but doesn't process—the copper and precious metals. It also deals in high-end metals, including dollar wafers and palladium at $800 an ounce. Metal leaches out of computers in unlikely places to the layperson. Monitor glass has lead in it, but monitors can't be processed like other computer parts and require a specialist extraction. But elsewhere at the plant, bits and pieces of computer trundle along conveyor belts, are ground down and shoveled into furnaces.

Jim Nelson is Settlements Manager for the Micro Metallics Corporation, part of the Noranda group. He takes me through the process of salvaging metal from the circuit boards, motherboards, and integrated circuits. Unlike Hackett's, this company looks for raw materials, rather than component parts that can be reutilized.

Noranda has been recycling for seventy years, but the combined factors of tougher environmental laws on landfill sites and the greater numbers of discarded computers have given the company a significant role in the Silicon Valley technology cycle. Typical lots range from 500 pounds to 40,000 pounds of material. They include monitors and keyboards, solder dross, router powder, gold pins, computer breakage, circuit board trim, plastic and ceramic ICs, precious metal sludge, printed circuit boards, sweeps, and wipes.

Here, circuit boards are processed by the thousands. Copper worked into components in southeast Asia traverses the globe, only to be scrapped, transported to Canada, and shipped out again as metal to Korea and Malaysia.

This is a hard hat and protective glasses environment. And Micro Metallics operates a Hazardous Waste Treatment and Storage Facility, checking material for radiation. Upstate in Roseville, Micro Metallics has a hardware disassembly plant.

The reprocessing cycle in San Jose goes something like this: shredder, hammer mill, Gilson splitter, tray furnace, ball mill—which grinds the two categories of residue into sweeps and metallics. An oscillating Sweco Screen separates out the metallics. These go into a gas furnace where the metallic pieces are diluted with copper to form what is called in the trade "a homogeneous melt." Samples are taken before the metal is cast.

Meanwhile the other bits, the sweeps, go into a rotary divider, a riffle divider, and a pulverizer. One last go back into the riffle divider and the sweep is all set to be processed as a laboratory sample.

Jim opens a door to show me a kind of alchemist's den. Old-fashioned balance scales are used to measure the increments of metal content to estimate value. In the end, customers' unwanted hardware is represented by samples of dust containing microscopic metal residues. These are poured into bags, labeled, and sent to Canada for evaluation.

In a climate of technological change—with an estimated turnaround for a new product of six months—recycling is a boom business. But it's a process confounded by the success of the industry it serves. As Silicon Valley's new technology accelerates, lands costs rise and a number of recyclers have been put out of business.

In a dumpster, the rain spatters on the plastic packaging of hundreds of unused circuit boards awaiting their end in the shredder and furnace. These have gone straight from production to discard. No useful life. Merely surplus to requirement.

Partners in Blue. A novel by Joseph L. Bean.
Chapter one

That's it. All that Phyllis Carraher knows of her father's book. The rest of the text is trapped inside Joseph L. Bean's old computer, on a software program that can't be read. The computer is called Herbie, and it now lodges in Sellam Ismail's warehouse. He is trying to find a way to access the data and print out the text.

On the phone from the mountain community of Senora, California, Phyllis Carraher tells me the tale of the lost novel. "My father is a retired Oakland police officer. He was a fabulous storyteller. He always told us stories when we were young and he had one book published by a vanity press. Then he was advised to write about what he knows best. And that's what *Partners in Blue* is about."

The problem is that Joseph, in poor health at 76, last typed around twenty years ago. The computer keyboard failed, a cruel irony for a man who used to own a typewriter repair business. Then he became ill, and the writing stopped. The machine lay idle, as technology changed all around it. Today Joseph can't remember much of the plot of *Partners in Blue,* and there's no print-out. But Phyllis found out about the novel's existence and was determined to resurrect it.

"It was time to scrap Herbie, and we were literally about to take it to the dump. Then some younger family members came over from Colorado and begged us not to throw the machine away, but to find a home for it." A seventeen-year-old niece discovered Sellam on the Internet and Phyllis found not only someone interested in the computer, but what was locked inside it.

"We figured he was our only hope. Dad was a bit teary when Herbie was taken away, but at least we have a chance of getting at the novel. We understand there's some family genealogy on there too."

But before he gets to that project, Sellam has a few more ghosts to raise. There's some Guatamalan geophysical data on eight-inch disks for starters. It's a complicated business, but deals with material less than twenty years old. It started when a geophysicist in Utah contacted Sellam about some lost data of 1980s land formations that had been plotted and stored on discs for an old NEC computer. He did not know the format of the data or what was on the discs. When Sellam tried one operating system there was no information on the disks—either they were in a different format or files had been deleted, leaving only the title on the outside of the disk. In theory, he says, it is still possible to recover these extinct files, even if the directory entry reads "file deleted." If they do still exist, Sellam will have to reconstruct the operating system to get them in some readable format. The trail will eventually lead to former NEC engineers "and finding people who know people." The only clue he has to go on is the type of disk—PC-8886 format, mid-'80s.

Lost data on punchcards is another area of data retrieval. But these at least are tangible. Later, Sellam emails me with an update. "On the disks with the geophysical data for Guatemala, I was able

to determine with the help of Fred Cisin and Don Maslin (a collector and archiver in San Diego) that the disks do still hold the data
but that we don't have the correct operating system to read them.
I'm still looking for the operating system."

Other ghosts materialize when Sellam is called in by attorneys
working on patent cases. He loans out old hardware so that a technological sequence can be surmised and a case made for a prior
patent.

So, what does become of data when it is deleted? Having lost
several thousand words of this text through "saving" glitches, I
wonder what form it now takes in the atmosphere. Strings of letters snagging on other people's lost words? An Aurora Borealis of
sentences and paragraphs, cascading through cyberspace?

Sellam sends me another file on the subject of accessing data. I
go to open it. It's completely in code.

ì¥Á7

    ð_¿

X_ bjbjUU

"-7|7|X
ÿÿÿÿÿÿÿÿÿl^^^^^^^_ªîîîî

THE NEWEST NEW THING |

. . . Americans, who participate in the world's most intense consumer
society, seem to possess an arsenal of indigenous theories that
account—in general terms—for the comings and goings of consumer
products. . . ."
—Michael J. Schiffer, *The Material Life of Human Beings*

Three weeks to Christmas and a succession of SUVs sweeps
through downtown Saratoga all bearing huge trees strapped to
their roof-racks. In the Santa Cruz mountains, the sports utility
vehicles come into their own for a seasonal family ritual. The
mountains are laced with Christmas tree farms. Find your favorite
tree, chop it down, load it up. In Los Gatos there are children
dressed as pixies. Householders turn a deaf ear to the persistent
warnings of power blackouts by playing join-the-dots with festive
light bulbs. Here, the outline of a house. There, a tree. On the
radio, the jolly carol subversion of "Walking in a Winter Wonder-
land" (called "Wandering Round in Women's Underwear") has its
first airing. This is the season of seemingly apocryphal tales that I
believe to be true.

Fry's store. Christmas Day minus twenty-three days. A store
worker addresses a group of around sixty customers about the like-

lihood that a truck full of Sony Playstations will arrive. Only the likelihood mind you. The Stanford Mall is heaving. Among the more unusual luxury items—a body lotion perfumed with essence of "dirt." Last year's ubiquitous gimmick gift item—a singing and talking fish—is still hanging on, though slashed to $5.

And the *San Jose Mercury News* reports that even in these tight times for Silicon Valley, there are some big parties going on out there. It's certainly one way to forget the election.

Smaller, neater, faster, cooler. Futurist and retro. On television I see a new mobile phone that is faced in wood. The way forward is sometimes the way back.

In the traditional Japanese setting of Hamasushi off Steven's Creek Boulevard, I have lunch with computer chip pioneer, Carver Mead. He is a pastmaster on all things new. He holds fifty patents

Carver Mead with the Foveon X3 sensor and Sigma SD9 camera. Photo courtesy of Foveon.

and won the 1999 Lemelson-MIT award, an honor given to a living American who has significantly contributed to society through invention.

A few weeks back, at a digital photography show, in Las Vegas, I had seen Mead's revolutionary new studio camera, called the Foveon. In a place where many claims are made to innovation, the Foveon is a radical departure from what we associate with the word camera. It looks like a lens mounted onto a laptop, which is set on a tripod. And that's really just what it is. And then some. On the laptop's split screen are two images. One is the almost filmic quality image of the model as she moves, almost real-time. The second is her captured image, which is stored in the computer. The photographer advances the "film" by depressing a "shutter" as in a traditional camera. The scores of stored images can later be manipulated using software, and printed with an extraordinary detail and depth of field.

What makes the Foveon unique is the gizmo at its heart—the world's highest resolution complementary metal oxide semiconductor (CMOS) based image sensor. Foveon claims this 16.8-million pixel sensor has around fifty times the resolution of low-end consumer digital cameras. Foveon, which is based in Santa Clara, worked with National Semiconductor Corporation to produce the sensor. It has nearly seventy million transistors.

Carver Mead has brought a sensor to show me. It sits on the table, as elegant as the sushi. It's about the width of a California roll. I am trying to make sense of that statistic—seventy million transistors. Mead cuts through the tech specification: "It's a new intelligent image plane." The inspiration for the invention comes from nature—the retinas of different animals were studied and these concepts combined with ideas from the physics of light. "The retina is a really awesome computer system," says Carver. "It's hard to replicate all that a retina does."

What's interesting to me about this development is its "new-ness." How does one come up with something that can be held to be innovative in Silicon Valley? One way of defining the measure of a thing is how far it is off the main evolutionary path. In terms of early technology, one thing does lead to another—from looms to punch-cards to computer coding. Cameras become smaller, more refined, or adopt the digital age with replacements and adaptations to the original form. The Foveon's design, says Mead, is radically new, a quantum leap. "It's not in a technological cul-de-sac."

Some clues to Mead's thinking come in the personal preface of his *Collective Electrodynamics: Quantum Foundations of Electromagnetism* (MIT Press, 2000). It is a work sprinkled with quotes from two of his acknowledged heroes—Albert Einstein and Richard Feynman. Feynman was a professor of physics at Caltech when Mead arrived as a freshman in 1952. He pioneered conceptual physics in the face of formalism. Mead recalls a lecture Feynman gave in 1959—"There's Plenty of Room at the Bottom"—in which he discussed how things can be made much smaller than we ordinarily imagine. It inspired Mead's work on electron tunneling, which had ramifications for the emerging field of integrated circuits.

"My calculations were telling me that, contrary to current lore in the field, we could scale down the technology such that *everything got better.* The circuits got more complex, they ran faster, and they took less power—wow!"

Mead's excitement comes from the potential of concepts merged from separate conceptual spaces, advanced by Arthur Koestler in *The Act of Creation.* So, the coming together of physics, computer science, biology, and art—Mead is an accomplished photographer—are expressed in the Foveon, together with an unquenchable zeal to enlarge "the space of ideas."

Modeling from the retina seems like wiping the slate and starting over. I wonder whether the vast amount of information available in our lives detracts from the process of getting back to basics.

Reevaluating the blindingly obvious. Invention often comes out of a lack of things.

A few weeks later, I am reading *Robinson Crusoe* for the first time since childhood. I'm looking for Daniel Defoe's early eighteenth-century slant on technology, and survival without it. I find myself dwelling on the hero's adaptation to the simple life, his fashioning of basic tools and his discovery of the difference between desires and needs. I smile at his indulgence of a second home—a "country seat"—inland on the desert island. Beyond need, this material culture fulfills desire. The book turns out to be an appropriate choice. The same week a new IPO is launched. Transmeta—with its advanced new microchip, called "Crusoe."

THE UPSHOT

WORDS WITHOUT MANUALS |

Once upon a time, librarians in Silicon Valley used card catalogs to search for book titles and authors. That was in 1991. Eeons ago in SiVa terms.

In 1992 the first online computers were made available to staff at Santa Clara Public Library. In 1994, Mary Hanel tells me, she and her colleagues were introduced to something called "gopher" through a correspondence course. "We were told that the graphic interface was the way to go."

"We went to an internet class. It was academically orientated but really an early version of Yahoo!. There was an indexing site with these two young guys tapping into Stanford's reference library."

At that time the fledgling internet was the province of academics, geeks, and those working in information technology. Librarians developed loyalties to particular search engines. "We would communicate and give each other advice."

As Santa Clara's Local History Research Librarian, and working there through the boom in the Valley outside, Mary has observed the developments more keenly than most. "There was an amazing speed of change after the commercial companies were allowed to get involved."

By 1997, there was a computer at every staff desk in the library. Three years later, I am walking through to Mary's office past dozens of public users, heads down at terminals, tapping into the internet or online catalogs.

Libraries, once the antithesis of all that was fast-paced and driven, are reinventing themselves at the core of local online communities. "The library is at the fulcrum of the academic-public interface."

Mary says the pace outside has created new expectations of the library service—one more predictable innovation being online renewals. "People expect things quickly. They used to be happy with a two-week wait for an interlibrary loan, now that's too slow for business people. And readers want more than a publication citation, they want the full text. But I can find information so fast. I used to have five or six directories to check, now I can reference the whole of the United States—twenty-one million entries sorted into an index."

Ease of access to information has generated a boom in family history. "Genealogy has exploded, probably owing more to the internet than any other hobby. It's phenomenal," says Mary. "We can make public records available, state records, the material in the Santa Clara History Center. This access changes the relationship the public has with personal data. They can do their own research from a terminal."

Educational resources are changing, too. "People are thinking faster but have shorter attention spans. It's important that material is presented well on sites. Kids are multitasking, connecting laterally. They can't read too much text. They don't want an unabridged book, they ask for text on tape so they can listen while they get on with other things."

"Those who come in solely to use the internet are a different species to the regular user," says Mary. "We call them 'cyberians.'

People would come in for the whole day if they could, but we limit them to one hour. They are the hard-core nerds and can be pretty asocial in a public space."

In keeping with Silicon Valley's tech-driven multiculturalism, the Santa Clara Library has Bollywood films in the video loans.

But some things don't change. People still come to the reference desk expecting the librarian to be the fount of all knowledge. One woman brought in a painting she'd bought at a flea market and wanted to know more about the artist. Mary checked a few websites and was able to oblige.

Another time she went to quiet down a trio of young boys who were giggling as they sat at neighboring computer terminals. "They were talking to each other, for sure," she said. "But not in the library. They were in the same chat room online!"

Santa Clara Library and the others of the fifteen cities keep a range of the wide literature published on the subject of computers and technology, and the history of Silicon Valley. It includes guide books charting the change from agriculture, to the stories of the big names and companies in the Valley—Intel, Netscape, Apple, Sun, Hewlett-Packard. More irreverent titles make fun of the hackers, the nerds, and the "Silicon Boys."

San Francisco musician and performance artist Thea Farhadian has her own take on Silicon Valley, garnered from working there as an assistant to a digital photographer taking images of data-processing technology. Farhadian's thoughts on the pace of life there inspired her to write a text that she performed in Berlin and San Francisco, against her own musical score. She plays violin. I listen to her tape as I'm driving down the freeway, the rush hour advancing in the fading light of the afternoon. Here is an extract:

> At one point, the photographer asks the art
> director, who is originally from Texas, "so how do you like

California?" and she says, "oh, i love it here, the
mountains, and the beach . . . and i love the fast pace
of San Francisco . . . one day my sister said, 'im moving
to California' and the next week i decided to join
her."
later in the afternoon im driving on the freeway to
this dot.com company to drop off a disk and
everybody is driving really fast and the cars are really shiny
and the streets are really clean and i hear the art
director say that in California everybody moves
really fast and they know what they want—they know how to
say what they want and they know how to get it. now.
so, as i keep thinking about how to support myself
as an artist, i think about joining this internet

"Thea Play Motion," digital image of Thea Farhadian. Photo by
Tom Upton.

> start up company. and as i think about joining this
> internet start up company, i get this really awkward feeling
> at the base of my neck and it travels down to my lower
> back and i imagine that where i really want to be
> is somewhere else. somewhere in another place,
> somewhere in another time . . .
> and this is what i think about and keep thinking
> about as i drive down the freeway.
> in Silicon Valley. (© Thea Farhadian 2000. Performed in San Francisco
>   and Berlin, 2000.)

Quotations run like data cable through one of the most comprehensive publications devoted to the Valley. *The Making of Silicon Valley: A One Hundred Year Renaissance,* edited by Ward Winslow, was published by the Santa Clara Historical Association with help from its Palo Alto counterparts. It lent its cultural theme to a television documentary about the Valley, narrated by Walter Cronkite. It is singularly concerned with charting success. "The constellation known as Silicon Valley represents the choicest achievements of America's high technology during the 20th century—a century in which the United States surged to world technological leadership and poured out inventions, innovations, and developments in a volume unprecedented in history, either in quantity or quality."

Scores of interviews were carried out and many of these were videotaped. The project produced a database of its time, enshrining the motivations of "a remarkable group of human beings." The list of grateful thanks in the preface is extensive. It also exposes Silicon Valley's cultural roots—"Dennis McNalley of The Grateful Dead arranged the use of musical excerpts as well as an interview with the late Jerry Garcia."

In October, Sellam Ismail auctioned an Apple-1 at the Vintage Computer Festival. I track down the purchaser, an Apple collector

Yumoto Hirohisa and Apple 1.

in Tokyo, and interview him by email. Yumoto Hirohisa's response is so enthusiastic, and says so much about the passion for collecting a particular machine, that with his permission I'm running it in full.

Thank you for your mail about Apple-1 auction.

1) Why did you want the Apple?

2) Do you collect computers?

As a matter of fact, I met Apple II computer in my student days about 20 years ago. In those days, there were not so many personal computers. And in those days personal computers' abilities were very poor.

One day, I wanted to use personal computer for my graduation thesis. And I asked my friend who is a computer expert. He said AppleII is the best machine for my purpose. And I bought AppleII plus. I was not a computer expert, but I learned programming by myself and I could make some programs. In those days, personal computer owners were rare and my friends at the university were surprised at the fast answers from my AppleII.

When I completed my graduation thesis, I used AppleII for programming and as a game machine. And I was charmed by the ability of this machine. I bought many games and other programs. Especially I was surprised at Adventure games like Sierra on the Line Adventure series. I loved the AppleII more and more. And I wanted to learn who made this great machine. So I started to research the history of Apple Computer Inc.

And I know two great Steves. I especially respect Woz, a genius. I know he made today's personal computer world.

His first work named Apple1 was the Big Bang of the personal computer world. Sure, Altair and IMSAI were released before Apple1. But Altair and IMSAI were not true personal computers, I think. They were only LED flash machines. I know Apple1 was the true first personal computer in the world.

I respect Woz and love the Apple machine, so I bought most kinds of the AppleII series, all kinds of Apple machines, all kinds of Lisa (Yes, I have Lisa1) and many Macs. And I gathered many peripherals, software and prototype machines and so on. And I gathered rival machines like Commodore Pet2001, TRS80, C-64, Atari, Amiga and NeXT, BeBox and so on. I have over 150 personal computers. But I have not so many Wintel machines.

I've been collecting because I VERY seriously want to build an Apple Museum in the future. So I bought an Apple1 in 1996, but the condition of this Apple 1 was not good. The motherboard was pattern-cut and the corner of the cassette interface was cut, by the first owner. Surely this is a lovely machine for me, but it is not good for the Museum.

So I saved money and I have been waiting for a day like this VCF auction. The Apple-1 I found at the VCF auction is in perfect condition and I want to get it absolutely.

3) Will you use it or put it on display?

I want to try to operate it, but after that I will put in on display in the Apple Computer Museum.

4) Has this realised a dream to own an Apple 1? Yes, of course. And I will display the great machine for everybody who loves personal computers.

5) Do you work in the computer field?

I am not in the personal computer industry now. But if Apple Computer Inc needs me for Apple Fellow, I will say YES. I know the history of Apple Computer and I have a vision for the Apple Computer of the future.

6) How old are you, and are you a family man? Do you collect anything else?

I am 42 years old. I am a family man. I collect only personal computers now.

P.S. On February 1988, I met Mr. Woz at the Mac World Expo in Tokyo. He shook hands with me and he said "Oh! My God," when he looked at my Apple1 photo.

He autographed my Red Book (first Apple II manual), Apple1 f manual, AppleIIGS and Powerbook 170 special edition. I was VERY pleased and cried over this big pleasure.

When I build an Apple Museum, I will invite him. Now I want to contact him. I tried at www.woz.org before, but I could not reach him because he was so busy. I want to talk with him. I respect him SO MUCH. I believe Woz is a true God in the personal computer world.

I will definitely build an Apple computer museum. So someone cooperate with me, it would be so much appreciated—

Best regards,

Hirohisa

More than words. Silicon Valley stories have a life of their own.

FINDING MEANING │

It's clear that Silicon Valley is developing into a two-tier society: those who have caught the technological wave and those who are left behind. This is not simply a phenomenon of class or race or age or the distribution of wealth—although those are all important factors. It's really about the Darwinian nature of unfettered capitalism when it's operating at warp speed.

—Jeff Goodell, "Down and Out in Silicon Valley," *Rolling Stone,* 1999, no. 827

Is Silicon Valley the rudest place on earth?

—Feature by Mark Emmons in *San Jose Mercury News* magazine, October 29, 2000

The *San Jose Mercury News* goes straight for the jugular. "Is civility being killed by people with too much money and too little time?" Incidents of road rage are increasing. One of the most disturbing incidents occurred in February, 2000, at San Jose International Airport. After a shunt a male driver reached into a female driver's car and threw her dog into the traffic, killing it. The man was later convicted.

Stan Mazor has been driving in California since he was sixteen. That's forty-three years. He tells me: "I always remember how gracious and courteous California drivers were. When I would drive in Boston or New York, I would always remark on how difficult the driving was compared to driving in California." Not so the case now. "There is a reduced level of courtesy as the traffic is more congested and competitive.

"Pedestrians used to have the right of way, but we must often wait in a crosswalk for drivers to stop. On our highways, drivers are hesitant to let us make lane changes when we are ahead and signaling a need to exit."

Four o'clock on a Thursday afternoon. I am driving in slow traffic on the 82 past San Jose when I notice a woman driver to my side who is forcing a path in front of me. As I begin to pull back to give her space, she scowls and gives me a variation on the finger sign. I am startled and give her more room, then have a hunch I should create even more space. I let two other cars in front of me as the traffic moves along. Within two minutes one of those cars has been forced onto the hard shoulder by the same vehicle. As that driver accelerates back into line, he scowls at the woman driver— and gesticulates.

Driving up the 101, I notice that a billboard lauding capitalism has been vandalized overnight by a fire. The damage has cut to the quick of the hoarding and leaves a kind of cigarette burn the size of a dining table. I wonder how my fellow drivers feel about the protest.

"The ancients understood science and technology as ways to pursue beauty, truth and goodness. And through most of history, technology served human ends. It's only in the last 20 or 30 years that we've done a flip-flop and that people increasingly have had to keep up with technology. . . . We're like a sleek Porsche that's cruising on the Autobahn at 150 miles per hour but there's nobody in the driver's seat. And the speed is accelerating." So says the technology writer Tom Mahon, interviewed in the *San Jose Mercury News,* October 28, 2000. He's talking about religion's role in a digital society.

On the face of it, Silicon Valley has plenty of religious practices. Often churches have multilingual notice boards advertising services in the same space to meet a variety of cultural groups. There are interfaith groups and nondenominational. The eastern and south Asian communities—Taoists, Buddhists, Hindus, Sikhs, Muslims—have mosques, temples, and prayer halls. There are synagogues and New Age spiritualist places for worship. Religion, it appears, brings community to a sometimes disparate group of tech workers and their families.

Even Eric S. Raymond's idea of hacker religion—"Agnostic. Atheist. Nonobservant Jewish. Neo-Pagan. Very commonly three or more of these are combined in the same person" (*New Hacker's Dictionary*)—is offset by the many notices for meetings of a spiritual kind that are advertised on notices and in the press of Silicon Valley. Episcopal/Anglican. Unitarian Universalist. Lutheran. Bahai. Center for Spiritual Enlightenment.

I recall the many deities worshipped on the Greek island of Delos when it was at its most flourishing point. I contact Tom and ask what he thinks is really happening. "In a nutshell it's about religion's fear of nature and nature's forces, and the desire to escape to another place; to heaven on high." He explains: "The Western religious tradition says that eating from the Tree of Knowledge— that is, doing science—brought about all suffering. Likewise, using technology to build the Tower of Babel brought about the confusion of language and community. Why would God give us minds and hands, then punish us for using them? I think the message was meant to be 'don't misuse your minds and hands,' but the lesson that comes down to us is, 'it can be sinful to use them at all.' And because this is our tradition, we have very few moral leaders now who know how to meaningfully address issues of science and technology. And the alternative is the emphasis on materialism, a bloodless spirituality that is counterproductive. We need to rediscover that doing science and technology is a sacred undertaking."

Sacred? Out on the freeways, actually getting to do science and technology in the Valley's pressure-cooker environment prompts something more like profanity. Bumper-to-bumper traffic has the knock-on effect of making people arrive at work—or home—with "an attitude." But what can we do? We can meditate, for one thing, says Mahon. "But people focus on coping. We should be looking at how we can use this rich portfolio of new technology to our own advantage. We are a ship without a rudder, and the rudder that directs this stuff should be kindness, concern, and compassion." And with a nod to the promise of an increasingly wireless world, a self-aware internet: "We haven't seen anything yet. If we are already disrupted by cell phones, how will we be when we have surgically implanted microprocessors? Are we ready to have our brains hacked into? Before this comes—and it may within our lifetime—we need an alternative vision. We have high-tech, why not kind-tech?"

The Sunday before Thanksgiving, and the *San Jose Mercury News* has a welter of weekend supplements for gifts, goodies, and otherwise decadent seasonal delights. Clothes, electronics, toys. The traditional Christmas spending frenzy begins apace.

But there's another supplement. It draws attention to other material things. Ten-dollar prepaid calling cards for instance. That would be a fine gift for senior sisters Lynn and Sammie Mayes. They live half a continent apart and haven't seen each other for eleven years. Those cards are on their wish list.

A new vinyl sofa and a love seat would bring comfort to the Sunrise Center in Santa Clara, where most of the elderly residents are of Chinese descent.

A $1800 hearing aid would transform the life of one Silicon Valley child. A $7 donation will give a San Jose senior center

Christmas dinner with trimmings. An $80 donation would treat residents of a shelter in Santa Clara to a pampering facial.

Computers, printers, and DSL internet access ($70) would transform a clubhouse for severely disadvantaged children on the wrong side of the "digital divide"; $429 would provide Zawdie, a young homeless man in San Jose with a bus pass. The wish list for an autism center includes metronomes at $67 each, a conga set ($329), and $15 tambourines.

Twenty dollars would provide replacement clothing for victims of rape whose clothes have been taken for evidence.

The Holiday Wish Book marked its seventeenth year in 2000. It is part of the holiday season in Silicon Valley and in 1999, $462,148 was raised for the causes and individuals featured. They have been chosen from the feedback of some five hundred social services agencies around the area. Contributions are tax-deductible. Readers can view the Wish Book stories and photos online and make a secure donation.

Jay Harris is the Publisher of the *San Jose Mercury News,* and officially one of the most powerful men in Silicon Valley. He receives me in his wood-paneled study, an anachronism to the rest of the newspaper building, but an elegant one at that.

Researching this book at times in the U.K., I read the *San Jose Mercury News* online. But it was only when I was stationed in the Valley for weeks at a time that I grasped the significance of the publication. It would be easy, one supposes, for a newspaper covering one of the most extraordinarily blessed and—up until now at least—upbeat places on the planet, to rest on its laurels and dole out a procession of success stories and back-slaps. But the *San Jose Mercury News* has a news mission statement:

> We are passionate about serving readers in Silicon Valley and its global electronic community, reporting and writing accurately and fairly,

shining a light on injustice and defending the public's right to know. We will reflect the changing demographics of the community in both coverage and hiring, recognizing that diversity is a core component of accuracy. Two stories are central to our mission: the impact of technology and the changing demographic landscape of America. These two stories create powerful connections between our community and others both domestic and international.

In other words, there is tech and there is nontech. But in an area the size of Silicon Valley symbiosis and grating up the wrong way are equally potential sources for stories. Harris gives me an overview of the newspaper's change over time. A commitment was made in 1995—the real boom-time in the Valley—to produce the best paper in America covering the technological changes and their repercussions. Staff were expanded, particularly covering high-tech; other bureaus were set up, and within two years the success of the *San Jose Mercury News* bred competition—*CNET, Zdnet, Wired.* Another upshot was that the paper's reporting staff were in great demand elsewhere.

Since then, the paper has continued to report rent atrocities as much as high-end development. Dot.bombs as well as dot.coms. Nontech stories, such as the uplifting section on celebrations, as well as the minutiae of the Valley tech scene. The paper is read not just in the Valley, as a regional daily, but globally as the cyberscene zeitgeist. "But not everyone who lives in Silicon Valley is affected by Silicon Valley," Harris reminds me. And not everyone in SiVa speaks American English. The *San Jose Mercury News* has published a Spanish edition since 1996, and a Vietnamese one since 1999.

FOREIGN CONNECTIONS |

[T]he economic prominence of the eastern Mediterranean area rested
upon a fortunate concurrence of a number of inventions occurring
within a few thousand years. These were copper, bronze, iron, the
alphabet, the horse, cattle, the wheel, and the boat. The peoples in
other parts of the world had no such happy concurrence on inventions.
Hence the Mediterranean peoples were given a tremendous lead over
the other peoples of the world by possessions of such a remarkable set
of great inventions.

—William F. Ogburn, "On Culture and Social Change," 1942

March, 2000. Six A.M., and Dr. Panayotis Chakidakis leaves his
home for the morning commute to his office. It's the same route
he's taken for more than fourteen years. He shares it with a few
goats. The new day stretches out before him. He pauses to notice a
new flower in bloom, gently raises its coral-colored petals. A sym-
phony of bees starts up as he continues down a foot-wide track,
stepping lightly on small, time-scattered pieces of marble, mosaic.
Beneath his feet are unexcavated Hellenistic houses. Over two
thousand years these former homes have lost their definition to the
naked eye and have merged with the uneven landscape. Panayotis
casts his eyes over ancient columns and down to the sea. All seems
well with his island.

Panayotis is the custodian and archaeologist of the museums on Delos and Mykonos. The islands lie at the heart of the Cyclades between Greece and what was once called Asia Minor. He chooses to live on Delos. "It has more light than anywhere else in the Aegean—light was born here." It is regarded as the birthplace of Apollo. The complex and changing fortunes of Delos since first habitation around 2000 B.C.E. made it a lure for archaeologists. Visitors, many from the United States, are also drawn to the beauty of a place that in its entirety is a cultural heritage site.

Since French archaeologists began excavations in the 1870s, only excavating archaeologists and museum workers have been allowed to stay overnight. Visitors arrive in the morning, stay five hours, and leave on the afternoon boats.

Panayotis has invited me to the island as his guest. I plan to stay one night, to experience first-hand the extraordinary still of the long late afternoon, and the journey into an antique night. But I am pressed for time, fitting this trip in between other research, a return to the United States, and my host's commitments. In the predictable pattern of my life, this will be a tight turnaround.

Arriving jaded off the morning boat, I find Panayotis supervising workers in a trench. They are excavating at the foot of stone pedestals, erected in the nineteenth century for the celebrated "Lions of Delos." The statues are being housed in the museum, and replicas put out on site. Panayotis wants to see what lies beneath the pedestals, an area as yet unexcavated. He looks up and, aware of my schedule, suggests I might not want to stay after all. The weather is looking bad and the boats may not come tomorrow. I look around me, and I'm already seduced by the place. I'm applying my brakes. "That's no problem—if it's OK with you?" "Sure! Let me show you where you'll be staying . . ."

We are walking up the track to a scatter of shepherd huts on a hillside. No cars here. The heavy stuff—containers of water, cans of olive oil, bags of vegetables, bottles of wine, tins of processed food—are all heaved off the shoppers' boats from Mykonos and brought up to the ten or so homes on the island. There are no shops. I've come with feta cheese, olives, tomatoes, yogurt, honey, water. A bottle of Scotch whisky for my host.

Panayotis tells me that since he came to the island he has lived in the same house. It is converted from a shepherd's hut, with a guest room attached. In the first of many conversations we have about modern life, Panayotis tells me he has all he needs. Until eight years ago, Delos had no electricity. No electricity to change the look of the island since ancient times. The nights were black and lit by the moon and stars. Panayotis read by candlelight. "The first time the security lights were on outside the museum, I thought it was a ship."

The island's water still comes from Mykonos. A water treatment plant might make it easier to bring development to the island. I've heard a casino rumored, at the least a hotel. That would change everything. There was a telephone in the Museum, and a fax machine. Panayotis had recently bought a laptop to continue research and writing at home, but he is alone with the technology. When his computer crashed he lost a year's work. Given the cost of phone connections, email, he says, is an unaffordable luxury. And on this speck of island, it is difficult to fully appreciate the difference such a taken-for-granted activity would make to life here. Through the internet, Panayotis could reach out to the world, but the world could also become a part of his island.

It is a contemplative life, but also one of splendid isolation. It is hard for Panayotis to leave the island—"I have to be there for it"—but in the beginning, the occasional nights in Mykonos kept him in touch with the world. His previous work had been at Delphi, home of another Sanctuary to Apollo. He regards himself as blessed to have also called that place "home."

Panayotis welcomes the tide of visitors and their questions. Most times, at least. He tries to educate as much about the island's past as how to preserve it for the future. Sometimes his patience is tried by people ignoring ropes and standing on delicate walls to get a better photography angle. It's two ways of seeing the past. The camera captures antiquity, as the visitor's foot crumbles it underfoot.

Then there is the academic work and museum administration, and plans for events to celebrate the island's unique qualities. There are festivals for children from the other islands who come in droves by boat and set the island ringing. "I am not lonely. Not really," he says, and the next evening, he would introduce me to some of his friends.

A simple supper, a welcome toast in Raki firewater, and deep sleep against the whistle of the wind. The effects of the Raki kick in, and I imagine Prospero on his island in a rage against the machine: " . . . deeper than did ever plummet sound, I'll drown my [Power]book. . . ." (*The Tempest,* act V, scene i).

I wake to the crash of shutters and doors. Panayotis has long since left for work. The wind overnight may have dislodged columns and he has a round of inspection. The sea is churning. I am stranded on Delos at the behest of the winds, the same inclement weather that turned classical writers green. Here, sheltered from the tempest, I have time to read and think.

When Panayotis returns, I offer to tidy myself up as we're going to meet his friends. "That won't be necessary," he says, setting off back down the path. As we walk, I grill him about the island's history. It's a built landscape of such unique preservation it is difficult to make sense of, even with a plan. The reuse of buildings from different time periods makes the use of archaeology central to understanding the cultural changes, and crucially, the rate of that change over time. Archaeological evidence can be reinforced by historical data. Classical writers, such as Thucydides, mention the fate of Delos in an account of war. Now lauded for its remote beauty, it was just as famed 2,500 years ago for being an economic and cultural nexus.

In Silicon Valley parlance, Delos was a boom town. Let's exchange the technological beat of the Valley for a force driving the ancient world—religion. The development of a place, such as Delos, as a votive center was significant for several reasons. There was an issue of "power." By word of mouth and mythological association, Delos had the power to draw people who hoped their actions would appease particular gods. They invested, by making offerings. They would need food and shelter, and therefore religious sites would help to promote trade. Witness the growth of pilgrimage sites such as Jerusalem, Rome, and Canterbury. Therefore, the control of such a site would be important in any attempt to seize power. As long as, that is, the same religion was practiced.

Delos has a number of significant sanctuaries and in the sixth and seventh centuries B.C.E. it was an important site for votive offerings. Its religious significance made it a valuable place to control. Several centuries of upheaval under a range of powers were halted by Delian independence under Philip the second of Macedon and Alexander the Great. From 314–166 B.C.E., Delos enjoyed rapid economic growth and freedom. By the third century B.C.E. it was a major center for the grain trade and banking. Archaeological evidence—objects from Roman, Phoenician, and Syrian cultures—suggests it was a truly international port. In 166 B.C.E., the defeat of Perseus of Macedon put Delos back in Athenian hands and they conceded it to the Romans. Old Delians were exiled, and the island was colonized by Athenians.

Delos was made a free port by the Romans, and it became the most important center for transit trade in the Aegean. Evidence suggests an ostentatious lifestyle on the island. It was cosmopolitan, with much oriental trade. The Athenians governed and the Romans regulated. The population grew to 25,000 by 100 B.C.E. But twelve years later, the island was looted after Delos remained loyal to Rome in war against the Pontic ruler, Mithradates. The population was killed or taken as slaves. In 69 B.C.E. destruction was completed by allies of Mithradates.

The Romans fortified the sanctuary and theater areas, but inhabitants were impoverished. Formerly opulent houses contained workshops. The Athenians tried to sell Delos, but there were no takers.

Over the next centuries, a small Christian community lived on the island, evidenced by the remains of an early basilica. Sundry visitors came and went, reporting the island to be deserted. In the eighteenth century, Delos began to feature in antiquarian records of ruins, and in "grand tour" travelers' drawings. In the nineteenth century, it appeared in photographs and guidebooks. By the time of the first French excavations it was well known as a significant site of antiquity. The Greek name of the islands in which it sits—the Cyclades—means those islands around Delos.

After the island's rising and falling fortunes, it is on the map in twenty-first century context. Panayotis agrees that it's now protected but he has fears for its future. Can the island exist in the twenty-first century without embracing it completely? We walk down close to the shore. The remains of the railway tracks left by nineteenth-century French archaeologists are on the surface, alongside lumps of marble and countless potshards. Old technology that was appropriate for the site. The tracks carried wagons of spoil from the excavation sites to the sea.

We're walking back inland, to a residential area where ancient houses are still standing. It's late afternoon and the wind's calmed. Inside the walls are warm. We move from one house to another. There are few physical boundaries. Only social ones. "I think you will like these people," Panayotis says suddenly. "One has to always respect that this is still their home." I realize that I am about to be introduced to a unique group of islanders. They died 2000 years ago. I sit on a stone bench in what would be the reception room of this villa. Panayotis paints a word picture of the inhabitants. "It's almost sundown, so they are preparing to have supper. The children are playing. Here, I found some toys . . ."

The light changes, illuminating here, casting shadows there. For a while, I am living on Delos in one of its golden ages . . .

Returning up the hill, Panayotis explains how he has "populated" the island by interleaving his archaeological finds with classical perceptions and gut feelings. There are houses he doesn't enjoy visiting, others where he feels he is welcomed as a friend. To call these people "ghosts" is simplistic. It's the response of someone to an environment that is almost free of twenty-first-century technology, and one in which the past is always present and unconcealed.

The wind picks up and is unabated for the next three nights and days. No boats can get in. But I am getting accustomed to the pace, and to the creativity required to prepare a meal with dwindling ingredients on a two-ring oven. We are scrabbling around in Panayotis's kitchen, looking for possibilities. There is no point asking the neighbor a hillside away—they are in the same position. It's ration time. Somehow we produce supper, and as we finish the meal and start talking about cooking in the ancient world, the lights go out. Panayotis reaches for a flashlight. He gets matches and lights a few candles. I take this chance to look outside at the blackness. I'm reaching for the poetic. It really is like black velvet shrouding the landscape. Under it, a succession of cultures. The moon illuminates some of the columns. The stars are all the more powerful for being reliably switched on.

It's a great time to be thinking about technology. Across the Aegean, on Mykonos—an acknowledged party island—the lights continue to tremble. On Delos, time does seem to stand still. A flash. The kitchen bulb is back in business. The refrigerator hums into life. Panayotis is relieved he hadn't been working at his laptop.

After six days, I wake to a calm sea. The morning is spent excavating some 3,000-year-old pottery and bringing it into the twenty-first century. Panayotis joins me on the afternoon shoppers' boat to Mykonos. It's another small island, but things are relative. It's a bustling place. It feels like a city. I resist looking for an internet café, and spend the evening thinking about archaeology and technology. I awake completely relaxed. So much so I nearly miss the first of a string of connections to return me to the U.K. I forget to forward my watch by an hour. Welcome to the world.

Iceland, February 2000. I am en route for Boston from London by Icelandair. The company allows a stopover in Reykjavíck, and we land in softly falling snow. Midafternoon, and it is practically dark. Apart from the glow of computer screens in shops, bars, café, and homes. Iceland has the highest per capita number of computers in the world. People tell me the internet has changed their lives. They feel connected to the world. They love it.

April 2000. The organizers of an international conference on computers and archaeology have accepted my paper on early technology. This will be my first airing of thoughts on computer collecting. Who collects, what they collect and why. The conference is in Ljubljana in Slovenia, an emerging country north of Croatia, on the Adriatic. To get there, I fly to Venice and take a couple of trains. Ljubljana is delightful. A river runs through it. I try to locate an internet café. I find one in a building that is a nightclub after dark. There are four terminals and a line of people. The service is free and there is no time limit. I am told I should just wait. This is the city's only public access to the internet. Later that day I fall into conversation with a couple from southern California. They now live in Italy, relocating for a change of life and pace. He is in the tech industry and says he can now work anywhere.

April 2000. A small hall on the outskirts of Munich in southern Germany. It's the location for the first Vintage Computer Festival in Europe. It attracts a sizable crowd over two days and networking is extensive. I talk to Helmut and Gaby, a couple who met and married through their mutual interest in old computers, looking for the email address of a CPM User Group. "I didn't believe a woman would want to be a member, " says Helmut, who heads the Amstrad enthusiasts' group in Germany. Computer collecting has a large following in Germany. It's helped by the floors of early technology history at the Deutsches Museum in Munich and at the Heinz Nixdorf Museum in Paderborn. The Nixdorf presents a cultural history of information technology over five thousand years—from cuneiform tablets to the present. Heinz Nixdorf was a computer pioneer and entrepreneur who died in 1986 leaving a collection of over 1000 historical objects. He nursed the idea of founding a museum to show people the story of computing. There are cyber trips through the Vatican at a software theater. Elsewhere, Silicon Valley has a dedicated exhibition. In another unrelated though complementary area, Digital Workbench visitors can watch a simulated traffic jam.

May 2000, Oxford. Sellam Ismail is hunting through the books at a charity store in a daze of delight. The redundant volumes and manuals are practically unobtainable in the United States. Most date from the 1970s and 1980s. They were made for British machines, such as the BBC computer, or present the emerging computer age from a British viewpoint. Given the time-lag in technological take-up—outside the scientific academic community—the books are cross-cultural history.

At Oxford University's computer services, I am asking about archived material relating to the academic use of the internet. I look at a batch of print-outs relating to a humanities program called Humbul. The paper is yellowing and I view it like an ancient artifact, a piece of papyrus or hammered vellum. It announces—"First foreign user, Hooray!" The date is 1988.

I am reminded that when I was working on my thesis at Oxford, I took several jobs to keep me going. One was a gift. For a few weeks I was a medieval manuscript foliator at my college, The Queen's, whose past members include the Web's creator, Tim Berners-Lee. The college library has one of the richest book collections in Britain. My work, such as it can be called, was to pencil-number the folios of some fifteenth- and sixteenth-century bound volumes. Some came from the library of Henry VIII, and may well have been held by him as he read. At the end of my shift, I would head back to my terminal, and log on to the internet. At my fingertips, two degrees of separation between Henry VIII and the inventor of the World Wide Web.

September 2000. In Lisbon for an archaeology conference, and nearing the end of this book's research, I need to keep in touch with Silicon Valley. I try to find an internet café. As with Ljubljana, they are thin on the ground. I'm directed to a cultural resource office in a pretty, old building near the center of town. The worn stone steps are lined with eighteenth-century tiles. At the top is a locked door with a buzzer. I ring to be admitted to what feels like an inner sanctum of a secret sect. There's a library and a few terminals. I wait for half an hour, bag my seat, and find the system is down.

IS THIS IT? |

Today, we face an explosive growth of knowledge; by any measure, our knowledge base is doubling every few years. How do we, as a human culture, prepare ourselves and our children for this world in which the knowledge base turns over many times within a single lifetime?
—Carver A. Mead, from remarks upon acceptance of the 1999 Lemelson-MIT Prize, April 22, 1999, San Francisco (published as foreword to *Collective Electrodynamics: Quantum Foundations of Electromagnetism,* MIT Press, 2000)

October 2000, The Golden Wok restaurant, Mountain View. I'm at a speaker lunch organized by TASC, a group formed out of a mission to mediate two key knowledge bases in Silicon Valley during the earlier wave of change. The subject today is mind over matter. The room is packed with some great character faces and I get to wonder the role of these people, most of them scientists, in the Silicon Valley story.

"I'm not even sure when TASC formed, but I was there." Dennis Paull tells me the background. "It was in '80 or '81 when the Midpeninsula Conversion Project in Mountain View had a grant to try to bring an understanding between the 'new technologists' and the indigenous population that was mainly rural/agriculturally based. This was done through four regional public meetings held in various areas of the county. Panels of technologists and others discussed what the new technology was, who the workers were, and how we all had similar concerns about social problems.

"TASC was formed by several of the 'tech' members of these panels and focused on the problems of those who were the subject of the recession in the military/industrial industries that was making things difficult at that time. We tried to help each other, but as conditions improved, only the biweekly luncheons continued. We have had about twenty-five luncheons a year for almost twenty years with a wide variety of speakers on a very eclectic range of topics."

Somewhat tellingly, he adds: "Of course, most of those original folks are long gone now, forced out by high living expenses and congestion."

The Midpeninsula Conversion Project changed its name to the Center for Economic Conversion. It is still in Mountain View. Its main focus is the transition by companies and individuals from government and military work to the commercial sector.

Stan Mazor emails me with a thought.

I came to Fairchild Semiconductor in 1964, and we used internal mail envelopes to send messages, which we normally had typed by a secretary:

day 1 draft to secretary

day 2 draft back for approval and changes

day 3 revised draft to secretary

day 4 final in internal mail to co-worker

response was by phone or similar cycle for return.

I was at Intel in 1969 the cycle was similar, but because of numerous remote sites the internal mail delivery took 2 days.

"Is it possible to lead a simple life in Silicon Valley? Only if you have what it takes." Dara Colwell reports on the phenomenon of downshifting in *Metro,* July 27, 2000. Her interviewee addresses the implicit catch-22. "Voluntary simplicity can't be reached below a certain income," he says, acknowledging the irony: money buys freedom. Another free Bay Area newspaper, the *Guardian,* in the week of October 11–17 tackles a further, if universal, problem associated with high-earning and fast living in a pressure cooker— drugs. "Diary of a dot.com junkie" is a first-person account: "I have a high-paying job at an e-commerce site. I have stock options that should make me rich. And I'm a heroin addict. I just wish I'd never been introduced to this drug."

After four months, I finally catch up again with Tom Jackie-wicz. We meet for sushi and he tells me that he hardly goes out to eat anymore. He's now a freelance consultant and technical author. The money he hoped for from a venture capitalist didn't come through. He has simplified his life. He and his girlfriend like to stay in and cook, watch a video. He has plenty of tales of the new, new Valley. Like the one about the man who had a margin call on his house and had to give up his half-share in the company he founded. The bars where techies no longer ordered drinks "all round," and the techies for whom drink and pot had become a necessary evil. Tom reckoned the *San Jose Mercury News* ad—"A month ago you were a 28-year-old millionaire, now you're just 28"—was cruel, but pretty accurate.

And at twenty-four, he felt the pace of people catching up on him. He was watching younger techies with less experience work from a lesser skills base—and get away with it. He was probably also leaving his apartment where the monthly rent had risen $800 since he'd been there. He looked different, had lost a lot of weight, had a couple more tattoos, and had started smoking again. "Light ones." We head out to the street and get into the Jaguar. Tom says he hardly ever takes his Jag on the road. Driving in Silicon Valley wasn't a cool experience. Back in Phoenix, where his family live, people reckoned twenty-five miles an hour to be "rush hour" traffic flow.

It's not yet 2 P.M. and we are already evaluating if we can make it over to Buck's Diner for coffee. We decide to risk it, but the traffic is advancing. The witching hour approaches. We get to Woodside, gulp a brew, dash back out to the freeway. It's a tad after 3:30 P.M. and the start of rush hour. Tom smiles. Ever the optimist. Whatever, he was planning on staying in Silicon Valley for another year at least. He reckoned there had to be a turnaround, it was still kind of exciting, and he wasn't ready to quit.

AN ARCHAEOLOGICAL TEXT |

U.S. Election Day, 2000. I've just called up an internet site run by writer, artist, and web-designer Robert Arnold. Apart from its sharp election comment and humor, www.DarkHorse2000.com is packed with information on the "third parties"—that is, not the Democrats or Republicans.

DarkHorse2000 was compiled as a field guide. Its website advises: "Some of the third parties are serious contenders, some not so serious, some are definitely playing out there in the fields of weirdness. As to which are which . . . well that all depends on where you're coming from." Many of the contenders had party descriptions linked to their websites.

And there are around 100 of them listed. Selecting at random I find the Free Pony and Ice Cream Party, the Lettuce Party, Cool Moose Party, Pot Party, Sunny and Share Party, Utopian Anarchist Party, Boring Party, American Beer Drinkers Party, National Barking Spider, and the Pansexual Peace Party. There's also a list of "lost parties" recognized in 1996 but unheard of since then. Among them, the Looking Back Party and the Coctail (*sic*) Party.

The U.K.'s far-side alternatives could hardly better the Raving Monster Loony Party. It was a regular feature in British politics until the demise of its leading candidate, Screaming Lord Sutch.

The content of the slick and witty DarkHorse2000 site was written by Robert and a team of writers. I first interviewed Robert back in the summer. He turned out to be another early computer enthusiast, with a background in the antiques and collectibles market. In fact he used to work as an art restorer at the Metropolitan Museum in New York.

He and his wife Sharna have one of those San Francisco homes that begs a catalog. Lots of fascinating objects, garnered from a range of time periods and contexts. Our conversation leaps around so much my notes are indecipherable.

On this election night, I email Robert. I ask what will happen to the site tomorrow, after the winner's announced.

U.S. Election Day, 2000 plus 2 weeks. Against considerable odds, DarkHorse2000 is still a viable site. The American constitution creaks and groans through Florida recounts, and the word of the year is "chad."

I get a message back from Robert. He and his wife have moved to more affordable Petaluma. He's looking at setting up an exciting new project. "We're planning to expand into a coalition of sites that covered local and regional politics—USVoters.com—but the development of the project is dependent on getting some sort of funding or sponsorship." In the meantime he's developing other sites.

December 12, 2000. I reopen this file and excavate the contents. The opening text is about election day. I remember writing it from an office in Saratoga, about 9 P.M. The television is streaming nonstop comment and speculation. The vote tallies are on the screen. The color-coded map of the United States shows Gore holding the coasts, Bush the heartland in between. Florida has yet to declare. The commentator suggests parents might want to wake their children and bring them to the screen—the tally shows Gore and Bush neck-and-neck. I call a friend and urge him to come look.

The next chunk of text was written two weeks after election day. There's a new business in my office space. The American public is on tenterhooks. The stock market is showing its discomfort. No one can quite believe this has dragged on for two whole weeks.

Writing this, nearly five weeks after the election, and the day before I return to the U.K. A news report this morning suggests a recession is more likely than not in 2001. The presidency is still unresolved.

December 13. It's all over. Al Gore concedes to George W. Bush. If the U.S. public is "bushed" by the battle—some might also say "gored" . . .

LOGGING OFF |

Can I remind passengers that smoking is forbidden in the toilets.
Anyone found doing so will be put out on the wing, where if they can
light it, they can smoke it!
—Part of the repartee of a Cabin Crew member, Virgin Atlantic flight,
San Francisco to London, December 13, 2000

In the manner of an archaeologist leaving an excavation site at the
end of a season, I am on my way out of Silicon Valley. The flight
back to London takes just under ten hours, and the mulling-over
time prepares me for this last document charting a year living on
the edge of technology, lifestyle, interactions. The drama, in the
end, was up close and personal. My site was one of the most culturally diverse and divided places I have ever visited. In India, the
outsider is prepared for the whack of emotion as stunning beauty
and striking poverty rivet the retina and then challenge the eye to
turn away. In Silicon Valley, sensibilities are blasted by hindsight.
The sheer keeping-up with the newness, moment by moment, is a
challenge that both exhilarates and exhausts.

In the embedded system that is Silicon Valley culture there is
little escape. And those who live there have developed a value
system that upholds the intensity of change. This is no place for

anyone who doubts what they are doing there. Pause to take stock and you may lose your footing. The only way I could write this summing up was to leave. Not for long, maybe. But to get a perspective that comes from a life lived a little less seriously. The decompression began on the plane, the piece of metalwork and vision that enabled me to commute between the Old World and the New. The Chief Purser on the flight laced his safety routine with wry comments that grabbed even the most jaded travelers' attention. This was still about technology, sharp rather than sharpest end. He also said something that made us laugh about the improbability of being shot through the air at great speed. A bit like the silver cigars streaking down the track at the Box Car Derby.

As the plane circles the skies over southern England, I look down to try to see archaeological features—the circles of Iron Age settlement, the lines of Roman foundations, and demarcations and scars of later histories. I remember the artist David Middlebrook comparing Santa Clara Valley orchards seen in photographs with the look of silicon chips—an idea he incorporated in a public artwork for San Jose airport. Now, as London comes recognizably into view, I see the squares and rectangles of housing estates, allotments, garages, the lines of railway and motorway—and I see integrated circuits. The plane banks, and the glass and plastics far below catch the sun like so many bits at the tech recyclers.

My last two interviews in Silicon Valley were two of the most powerful, in different ways. I talked for a long while with Tom Mahon about how people adapt to change in a place where time-to-market is a mantra. We shared anecdotes about the wired world. He told me about a retreat he'd organized two years ago for techies who had expressed an interest in unwinding. Noone came. Not enough time. I told him about an attempt to get to a meditation class that was thwarted by a three-hour journey in traffic after which I was more stressed than when I set out. We tutted about the rush-hour, the incivility, the housing costs, the way the stress spreads globally through software bugs caused by the pressure to produce new products, the way of disengaging with reality that seems peculiar to Silicon Valley. Then we realized this wasn't too helpful. Technology in whatever form exists, it accelerates, it won't go away. "It's time to find a way to deal with it," says Tom, who's onto something. This time he thinks the moment is right. "The San Francisco Bay Area is the Western terminus of western civ; the end of a 10,000 year march westward that started in the Fertile Crescent. In the last 50 years here, we've developed the atom smasher, the gene machine, the microprocessor, artificial intelligence, biochips . . . But what for, where to from here?"

Later that day I ring a number in Sri Lanka. Buzz, crackle . . . the connection is made. An English man answers and two voices later I am speaking to Arthur C. Clarke, the man who for me, and countless others, made computers come alive. The images of early man, old tools, and new technology meeting in *2001: A Space Odyssey* dwelt in my mind for more than thirty years. In some way, they come together in this book.

Arthur had been primed of my interest by Heather Couper, an astronomer friend of mine who knows him well. But a film crew has just left and Arthur suggests I fax him instead. Fax? I think. Seems antiquated and slow . . . email? I venture. I can hear Arthur's sigh rock the calm of old Ceylon. "No, no, I have so many these days I simply can't cope with them. In fact, I want it to be cut off . . ." We are noting the irony. On the cusp of the year he has made his own, Arthur C. Clarke—who brought us the possibility of robots, personal interaction with technology, the frisson of the visionary's gaze—wants little more than some old, old thing.

EPILOGUE |

We worked in those mines, waiting for our golden years. Well, now it's
our golden years, and it's done nothing but cost us gold. This is no way
to live.

—Former uranium miner, Jack Beeson, who has a lung disease and was
waiting for Congress to resume compensation, quoted in the *New York
Times,* March 28, 2000

June 1, 2001. In the six months since completing the text of this
book and awaiting the final page proofs, change over time has
continued in Silicon Valley. Out of their context, Jack Beeson's
words might apply to the dot.comers who came with dreams and
are left with thirty-five working years ahead of them.

Rather than touch the content of this book as I completed it in
January 2001, I have chosen to leave it as a sealed context, in itself
an archaeological term that relates to a place such as a tomb, or the
area under a known geological event, such as a rockfall, which can
be assumed to leave evidence beneath intact, if damaged.

As the NASDAQ continued to plunge—down 3000 points
from its high of 5048 on March 10, 2000—the fall-out from the
dot.com demise became palpable in the very things I'd observed on
the up. Thousands of job losses, the evaporation of virtual millions,

a Gold Rush–reversal of migrations back across the States, returnees overseas who left their home cultures as heroes, deprived of both jobs and H1Bs. Significant moves and shakes include the resignation of Jay Harris as publisher of the *San Jose Mercury News* over job cuts early in the year; Dag Spicer's departure from The Computer Museum History Center; Leonard Hoops leaving his marketing eyrie in Silicon Valley for a new role in Sacramento. Tom Jackiewicz, meanwhile, has taken his mantlepiece curiosities to a new apartment and he is now a tech.contract worker; his white-hot coding pal, Adam, took a break from the industry and moved to the Santa Cruz Mountains.

In a nod to the electricity crisis, the Yahoo! sign near San Francisco is turned off at night. It now reads "Here, take my electricity"; the Apple sign on the other carriageway has graffiti that reads "Now What?"

The *San Jose Mercury News* has an online reader forum on the affects of the downturn; there are large numbers of this-year and last-year registered Porsches in its "for sale" ads, and there is markedly less traffic on the Silicon Valley freeways. Sellam Ismail has moved his vintage computers to another warehouse; his previous one has new life as apartments. The recycling business now extends to nonvirtual auctions of dot.com material culture.

Business rents have fallen steeply; residential rents look set to follow when contracts are negotiated. There are signs reading "Apartment to let," great numbers of "For sale" boards—and I saw "Price Reduced" on one house in the Rose Garden, San Jose.

On my first visit back for five months, I took the train down to San Jose from Oakland, sat in a coffee shop, read the *San Jose Mercury News,* and felt something different in the air. Despite the economic downturn there was an energy about the place. People talked to me of a sense of relief. At a cinema in San Jose I watched a documentary called "Secrets of Silicon Valley" and the audience groaned with hindsight.

My own tail-chasing—and tale-chasing—in Silicon Valley continues as the pages of this book are printed, and beyond. I'm hooked on this place. I can watch time work its changes.

Over brunch in Atherton, I remarked to Carver Mead that I felt I'd lived through the rise and fall of the Roman Empire in a single year. He corrected me, saying the last five years was an inflated and unnatural state for Silicon Valley. A Rubicon had been crossed, it seemed, but there had been no demise. It had always been more than the dot.coms.

He leaned back, eyes twinkling. Now we'd see what Silicon Valley was really all about.

As with so much of this book, ideas for further reading changed considerably over the year of research and writing. The planned academic footnotes and citations became overly specific; instead what follows is a more general reading list on the subjects discussed in this book. As shown by the works cited in the previous pages, my sources ranged from eclectic texts to electronic narratives and down-to-earth hard-news reports. However, these are all ideas of tangible texts; the internet offers up a whole new world of possibilities.

There is an extensive range of publications that chart the rise and rise of twentieth-century Silicon Valley as a center of technological excellence. Most are grounded in the local history—the development of Stanford and the commercial impetus resulting from the other established industries, such as lumber and fruit orchards. There are two waves of publications, reflecting the two-pronged dynamic of Silicon Valley—the early tech boom of the 1960s to 1980s, and the internet-driven economy of the 1990s. The publication dates speak volumes about the author's likely take on the highs and lows of Silicon Valley, while the second edition of *Fire in the Valley: The Making of the Personal Computer* (2000) begs comparison with the first, substantially slimmer version, as an example of change over time.

The Place
John Steinbeck lived in Monte Sereno, an eyeblink of a city near Los Gatos, and his true Californian epic, *The Grapes of Wrath,* bookends the newer narratives. *The Making of Silicon Valley: A One Hundred Year Renaissance,* edited by Ward Winslow (1995), is a classic text, tracing the development of the industry from the

building of Stanford University and the earliest start-ups. Narrowing the focus, Silicon Valley's many historical associations produce publications that are based on insider knowledge. They include Clyde Arbuckle's *History of San Jose* (1986); Jack Douglas's *Historical Footnotes of Santa Clara Valley* (1993); Yvonne Jacobson's *Passing Farms, Enduring Values: California's Santa Clara Valley* (1984); Jeanette Watson's *Campbell: The Orchard City* (1989); and Willys Peck's *Saratoga Stereopticon: A Magic Lantern of Memory* (1998). Marvin Cheek's *Silicon Valley Handbook* (2000) is a comprehensive segue between old places and high tech. Annalee Saxenian's classic study of Silicon Valley and its East Coast counterpart *Regional Advantage: Culture and Competition in Silicon Valley and Route 128* (second edition 1996) is a crucial text for understanding the West Coast's high-tech boom out of the counter-culture movement. On a global scale, innovation uptake in the Western world is examined by Jared Diamond in an acclaimed fusion of science and history, *Guns, Germs, and Steel* (1998).

In theoretical terms, photographic and poetic response to "place" is one of the considerations in Michael Shanks's influential *Experiencing Archaeology* (1992). See also R. H. Thompson's paper, "The Subjective Element in Archaeological Inference," in the *Southwest Journal of Anthropology* (12).

The People

People and how they relate to things—whether computers, cars, or houses—is a recurrent theme of this book. In terms of archaeology, this is an approach under the umbrella terms of material culture studies. The study of objects has already produced some classic works. Pioneers in the field include Ian Hodder, whose *The Meaning of Things: Material Culture and Symbolic Expression* (1989) informed a generation of archaeologists. *The Social Life of Things* edited by Aaron Appadurai (1986) is an exemplary series of essays.

See also *The World of Goods* by Mary Douglas and B. Isherwood (1979); *The Practice of Everyday Life* by Michael De Certeau (1984) Daniel Miller's *Material Culture and Mass Consumption* (1987); Marvin Harris's *The Nature of Cultural Things* (1964); and Henry Hodges's *Artifacts: An Introduction to Early Materials and Technology* (second edition 1976), which is utterly absorbing. *The Material Life of Human Beings: Artifacts, Behaviour, and Communication* by Michael Schiffer with Andrea Schiffer (1999) is the latest in a theme that includes *Formation Processes of the Archaeological Record* (1987).

Middens and rubbish pits are valuable elements of excavated data. For a consideration of depositions and their possible ritual significance in the ancient world, look at Barry Cunliffe's comprehensive volume, *Iron Age Communities in Britain* (third edition 1991). And compare with the remains of the modern American consumer society in *Rubbish! The Archaeology of Garbage* (1992) by U.S. archaeologist William Rathje with Cullen Murphy. See also Grant McCracken's *Culture and Consumption* (1988).

For a nonarchaeologist's perspective on material culture see *American Artifacts,* edited by Jules Prown and Kenneth Haltman (2000), or the essays in Tom Wolfe's *Hooking Up* (2000).

An invaluable reference is *Material Culture: A Research Guide* by Thomas Schlerith and Kenneth Ames (1985). For more on the use of more recent artifacts in the same way as traditionally excavated data, see the increasing range of historical archaeology publications such as *The Material Culture of Steamboat Passengers* by Annalies Corbin (2001), and my own research on the contemporary use of Chaco Canyon prehistoric site in the American southwest (in the journal *Antiquity,* 1998). A full account of the changing fate of the Mycenaean columns appears in the *Oxford Journal of Archaeology* (2001). Caroline Humphrey's "Inside a Mongolian Tent" is in *New Society,* 31 Oct. 1974.

A slim volume entitled *The Gift* by Marcel Mauss (1954) is
an anthropological classic. Its study of things given and received,
with the attendant baggage of reciprocity, is a cornerstone of social
economic theory. *Exchange Systems in Prehistory,* edited by Timothy
Earle and Jonathan Ericson (1977), is one of a range of archaeological works that examines objects and their users and suggests the
social activity associated with them. Objects observed in use informed the work of the anthropologist Marshall Sahlins in *Stone
Age Economics* (1972).

The image of a fictitious archaeologist's wife with a toilet seat
around her neck as an "adornment" is one of the enduring images
in the highly entertaining *Motel of the Mysteries* by David McCauley
(1979), which considers how future generations might perceive the
twentieth-century world. This gentle ribbing of Schliemann's
excavations is one of a number of inventive works that look at such
cultural icons as Disneyland and shopping malls as archaeological
sites.

The Tech

Paul E. Ceruzzi's *A History of Modern Computing* (1998) provides a
fine context for any study of the subject. The history of computing
is a rapidly growing field of research with significant contributors
within it who are framing and defining the Silicon Valley culture.
These include *Bootstrapping: Douglas Englebart, Co-worker, and the
Origins of Personal Computing,* Thierry Bardin's study of the inventor
of the "mouse" (2000).

The story of the tech object is necessarily one of people using,
developing, creating the objects. The hardware, software, and e-
economy histories make for varying narrative threads that are
invariably entwined. See *Technology in the Garden: Research Parks
and Economic Development* (1991) by Michael Luger and Harvey
Goldstein; *The Big Score: The Billion-Dollar Story of Silicon Valley*

(1985) by Michael Malone; *The New Alchemists: Silicon Valley and the Microelectronics Revolution* (1982) by Dirk Hansen; and Katherine Davis Fishman's *The Computer Establishment* (1981).

A growing number of biographies and autobiographies try to get a handle on the dynamic individuals at the heart of it all. Bill Gates is geographically north of the Valley, but his account of Microsoft's history *The Road Ahead* (1995), has a cast list that is significantly outside California. See also David Kaplan's *The Silicon Boys and Their Valley of Dreams* (1999) and *Sunburst: The Ascent of Sun Microsystems* by Mark Hall and John Barry (1990). Michael Lewis's *The New, New Thing* centers on Netscape and its founder Jim Clark, while David Packard's *The HP Way: How Bill Hewlett and I Built Our Company* (1995) is all the more poignant with the death this year of the second of the two HP founders. *Inside Intel: Andy Grove and the Rise of the World's Most Powerful Chip Company* (1997) by Tim Jackson complements Intel Corporation's museum in Santa Clara.

For an exercise in historical narrative, *West of Eden: The End of Innocence at Apple Computer* (1989) by Fran Rose should be read in sequence with Steven Levy's *Insanely Great: The Life and Times of the Macintosh, The Computer That Changed Everything* (1995); Michael Malone's *Infinite Loop: How the World's Most Insanely Great Computer Went Insane* (2000); and Alan Deutschman's *The Second Coming of Steve Jobs* (2000).

As a kind of archaeological enterprise, working through books by futurologists and the visions of early engineers is a rewarding exercise and gives weight to the rapid change over time in the tech world. Charity shops are good hunting grounds for these books, discarded as being out of date but actually having a new value for their historical perspective. Titles include Alvin Toffler's influential *Future Shock* (1970); Forest M. Mims's *Siliconnections: Coming of Age in the Electronic Era* (1986); *The Electronic Cottage: Everyday*

Living with Your Personal Computer in the 1980s by Joseph Deken (1982); Robert Heinlein's science fictional *Stranger in a Strange Land* (1975); and *Computers and the World of the Future,* edited by Martin Greenburger (1962). Mary Orna's *Cybernetics, Society, and the Church* (1969) and Thomas Whiteside's *Computer Capers: Tales of Electronic Thievery, Embezzlement, and Fraud* (1978) both predate cybercrime and morality checks imposed by the internet era.

A number of the corporations in Silicon Valley have their own archives, and computer museums as well as individual collectors keep written material such as manuals and other documentation. Stanford University houses the archive of Apple Computers.

The Upshot

Keeping a finger on the pulse in Silicon Valley is a combination of serious hunting and gathering, and serendipitous freeloading. Cultural osmosis also plays a major part. The crucial reading material on a regular basis includes a series of monthly journals—*The Industry Standard, Wired, Red Herring, Fast Company*—the daily and weekly press—*San Jose Mercury News, Palo Alto News, San Francisco Chronicle, Metro, The Guardian*—together with the *Silicon Valley Tech Week, The Business Journal, San Jose Magazine,* and *Gentry.*

In the space between inputting this text and its publication, I imagine it to be joined by a stream of titles charting the ebb and flow of Silicon Valley fortunes. At time of writing, the balance lies between Po Bronson's VC tales *The Relentless Pursuit of Connection* (1995); Guy Kawaski's *Computer Curmudgeon* (1992); *Charged Bodies: People Power, and Paradox in Silicon Valley* by Thomas Mahon (1985); Tim Jackson's *Startup: A Silicon Valley Adventure* (1995); and such titles as *Behind the Silicon Curtain: The Seduction of Work in a Lonely Era,* by Dennis Hayes (1989); *Microserfs* by Douglas Coupland (1996); Tracy Kidder's acclaimed account of 1970s high-tech pressures in *The Soul of a New Machine* (1997); and *Sunnyvale,* a skillful and sobering real-life narrative by Steve Goodell (2000). *Living at the Speed of Light: Your Survival Guide to Life on the Information Superhighway* (1994) by Danny Goodman, again (just) predates the internet boom.

John Naisbitt has charted technology since *Megatrends* in 1984 and his latest book is more reflective—*High Tech, High Touch: Technology and Our Search for Meaning* (1999). Similarly reflective, Nicholas Negroponte's elegant essays in *Being Digital* (1995) offer a history of media technology while flagging up the inherent drawbacks of technology dependency. Eric S. Raymond's *New Hacker's Dictionary* (1991; third edition 1996) is a classic, as is *The Computer and the Bazaar,* which addresses the question of open source and the development of the Linux operating system. Connie Hale and Jessie Scanlon's two editions of *Wired Style: Principles of English Usage in the Information Age* beg comparison for changes in linguistic vogue and epistemology (1997 and 1999).

For lighter relief, although the anecdotes have an edge, see Robert Cringley's epically titled *Accidental Empires: How the Boys of Silicon Valley Make Their Millions, Battle Foreign Competition, and Still Can't Get a Date* (1992/1996); while Po Bronson's *The First $20 Million Is Always the Hardest* (1997) and *The Nudist on the Late Shift* (1999) are more of the "only in Silicon Valley" stories pursued by *San Jose Mercury News* columnist Mike Cassidy. *Computing Across America* by biking computer nomad Steven K. Roberts (1988) offers an alternative perspective, in a travelogue that includes California.

And, by way of closure, Arthur C. Clarke's *2001: A Space Odyssey* (1968) has a 2001 edition.

xxiv

"Bunny suit." Courtesy Intel Corporation.

xxv

Great America, Santa Clara. Courtesy Santa Clara City Archive.

xxvi

Artifacts, Intel Museum, Santa Clara. Courtesy Intel Corporation.

xxvii

Mantle trinkets, Tom Jackiewicz's apartment, San Jose, January 2000. Photo by the author.

xxviii

Sculpture by David Middlebrook, Westin Hotel, Palo Alto. Courtesy David Middlebrook.

xxix

Artist with Apple ad, Los Angeles, May 2000. Photo by the author.

xxx

Familia-Y-Vida health mural, Alviso. Photo by the author.

xxxi

Bayside Canning Co., Alviso. Photo by the author.

xxxii

"Surgery Flat," Julieanne Kost. Courtesy Julieanne Kost/Adobe.

xxxiii

Painted Highway, Silicon Valley. Courtesy California Department of Transportation.

xxxiv

Rosicrucian Egyptian Museum, San Jose, September 2000. Photo by the author.

xxxv (top)

Entrance to the Rosicrucian Egyptian Museum, San Jose. Photo by the author.

xxxv (bottom left)

Mycenean columns, Treasury of Atreus, Greece, artist's impression, early twentieth century. From *1928 Guide to the Greek and Roman Antiquities of the British Museum.*

xxxv (bottom right)

Sistrum. Artifact number RC1765, Rosicrucian Egyptian Museum, San Jose. Courtesy Rosicrucian museum, San Jose.

xxxvi

Rosicrucian Egyptian Museum, San Jose. Photo by the author.

xxxvii

Fry's Electronics, store exterior, Campbell, May 2000. Photo by the author.

xxxviii

San Jose Mercury News ad: "Million dollar estate." Courtesy William Howard, Saatchi SF, and the *San Jose Mercury News.*

xxxix (top)

Old house, Alviso, August 2000. Photo by the author.

xxxix (middle)

House for sale, Hicks Road, Los Gatos. Courtesy Ian McRae.

xxxix (bottom)

Archive photograph, Alviso Yacht Club. Courtesy Historic
Collection, City of Santa Clara, California.

xl

Cover of Skinner's technology sale catalog, April 1, 2000. Courtesy
Skinner's, Boston.

xli

Ad for Honeywell's Kitchen Computer. Courtesy The Computer
History Museum Center.

xlii (top)

J. Presper Eckert (on left) with ring counter from ENIAC.
Courtesy Skinner's, Boston.

xlii (bottom)

J. Presper Eckert's slide rule. Courtesy Skinner's, Boston.

xliii (top)

DEC equipment and ephemera, John Lawson's house, Malibu
Hills. Photo by the author.

xliii (bottom)

Computer kit, from Sellam Ismail's vintage computer collection.
Photo by the author.

xliv

Recycling chute, San Jose. Courtesy Tony Cole.

xlv (top)

Cable, recycler's, San Jose. Courtesy Tony Cole.

xlv (bottom)

Recycled metal ingots. Courtesy Tony Cole.

xlvi (top)

Recycling chips. Courtesy Tony Cole.

xlvi (bottom)

Circuit boards, recycler's, San Jose. Courtesy Tony Cole.

xlvii

Salvaged gold pieces, recycler's, San Jose. Courtesy Tony Cole.

xlviii

San Jose Mercury News ad, 2000: "Millionaire." Courtesy William Howard, Saatchi SF, and the *San Jose Mercury News*.

xlix

Oak tree, San Jose, September 2000. Photo by the author.

3

Tom Jackiewicz, January 2000. Photo by the author.

11

"Witch in a bottle." Courtesy Pitt Rivers Museum, Oxford.

12

George Chiu, Palo Alto. Photo by Florence Chiu.

13

Dan and Nan Boyd, Palo Alto, May 2000. Photo by the author.

30

Early portrait of Ada Lovelace. Courtesy Ashfield District Council, Council Offices, Kirkby-in-Ashfield, Nottingham, UK.

34

Bruce Roberts, Silicon Valley, May 2000. Photo by the author.

58

Pacific Coast, near Silicon Valley, January 2000. Photo by the author.

94

From left: Tom Williams, Adam Lyons, and Tom Jackiewicz, downtown San Jose, January 2000. Photo by the author.

103

Scott and Cara France, San Francisco Airport. Courtesy Paul Mueller.

133

John C. Toole (left) and Dag Spicer, The Computer History Museum Center. Courtesy The Computer History Museum.

138

Jamis MacNiven, at Buck's Diner, Woodside.

140

Sellam Ismail, Oakland, January 2000. Photo by the author.

153

Marvin Johnston, Santa Barbara, May 2000. Photo by the author.

157

Nathan Myhrvold, computer collector, Seattle. Courtesy Nathan Myhrvold.

165

Recycling, with family photos visible. Courtesy Tony Cole.

175

Carver Mead with the Foveon X3 sensor and Sigma SD9 camera. Photo courtesy of Foveon.

183

"Thea Play Motion," digital image of Thea Farhadian. Courtesy Tom Upton.

185

Yumoto Hirohisa and Apple 1. Courtesy Yumoto Hirohisa.

INDEX

Silicon Valley continues to change, and so too do our responses to it. This book, as a text traveling through time, gathered a variety of reactions, from within and without its geographical heartland.

Within weeks of publication, *Artifacts* was offered, at premium price, as a collectible on Amazon's website. But it was a history book even as it was being written. As one reviewer mentioned, it is now an artifact in itself. It is therefore open to interpretation: Those who have disagreed with my (ab)use of archaeology, or questioned my outsider's survey techniques as being more like those of a vacationer, provide illuminating perspectives on preservation of each personal story, and the development of Silicon Valley—the myth.

As I write, the Valley is reeling from the dot.com demise, or more the rate of that demise. I hesitate, as by the time this is published, the economy will have shifted. But placing this afterword here, behind the index, helps draw a line underneath the excavated text and allows a helpful distance.

Around 80 percent of the material I drew on in 2000 could not be gathered now. From the clearer material culture of the tech boom, or the transition phase when the decline was seen as a glitch, the cultural patterns are harder to discern; people's lives appear more individuated and frag-mented. A form of mythmaking begins. As people have moved on, objects, displayed in new homes outside the Valley or dispersed on eBay, have a weight of trophy or souvenir. Events are tied to the minutiae of the mo-ment. Arrival in Silicon Valley, the date of a company's IPO, how quickly stock options were realized; how many companies worked for, how many start-ups.

The history of this time continues to be as multistranded as the analo-gies I drew between traditional archaeology and that pulsing digital age. When discussing the book with technologists, the nods and sighs revealed the cycle of the dot.com era to be just that. The youth of those involved in the boom years created an illusionary sense of eternal growth. The sages had long been waiting for the technological tide to change. As the economic slump set in during 2002, I was aware that some of those I was addressing felt distressed that what had been a reality was now history.

In my readings outside Silicon Valley but still on the West Coast, there would be those in the audience eager to validate the boom days anecdotes, who had left the Valley on a hunch. Further east, the stories took on an extra edge. The much called-on Silicon Valley hubris was recognized, and discussion dwelt time and again with Route 128 and "why there, not here?" As I read outside America, in Oxford or my seaside hometown in southeast England, the points and anecdotes took on a form almost of fiction. Audiences there are so far removed from the heartland of the text, that the stories become merged with other bold enterprises such as the tulip wars in seventeenth-century Netherlands. America is a foreign country, and for many, Silicon Valley and its hype have passed them by.

But one common factor affected all these audiences: the loss of orchards in Silicon Valley. The story of the Olson family is seen as epic and tragic. And despite its setting in the enduring epicenter of the high-tech world, it represents nothing less than a worldwide and historic phenomenon, the fight for the "old ways" in the way of the "new."

Whether tech workers or service workers, those I talked to have been forced to reshape their lives. Many are still looking for work. My response that they have watched history made is a lost and nonessential statement at this uncertain time.

Personal histories are forever tied to this extraordinary period of gain and loss. Those who were there will be aided by history, which ultimately helps us make sense of our world. The former dot.com millionaires have a new role, as much a part of the retelling of the Valley story as the semiconductor pioneers. When the new Computer Museum opens, there will rarely be a place of history so rich with the artifacts of so many contemporary lives.

May 2002